THE
ANALYTIC
DETECTIVE

THE
ANALYTIC
DETECTIVE

Decipher Your Company's Data Clues
and Become *Irreplaceable*

STEVE LEEDS

HOPECAST PUBLISHING
Hopecast, LLC 2021

http://www.hopecastpublishing.com

ISBN: 978-1-7373081-0-2 (print)
ISBN: 978-1-7373081-1-9 (ebook)

Ordering Information:

Special discounts are available on quantity purchases by corporations, associations, and others. Please go to http://www.hopecastpublishing.com for more details.

CONTENTS

INTRODUCTION

Ask anyone who loves analytics and they'll tell you that there's something very exciting about finding some pattern in data that no one has really noticed before and can actually be used to have a positive impact on the business. While marketing and sales teams are trying to figure out where they should put their effort and investment to keep the business growing, analytic groups are trying to find useful patterns buried in the different available company databases, and find a way to clearly summarize those findings. When they're all on the same page, speaking the same language, and the results are not only insightful, but actionable, you'll have a great experience on both sides. Moments like these are where analytics meets the business.

While all of this sounds like a great recipe for success, there is an all too common disconnect that occurs and creates frustration from those receiving the results of an analytic effort. Whether it's spoken aloud or just barely whispered under their breath in frustration, it's not unusual for them to say or think, "What should I do with all these reports, spreadsheets, and dashboards? What are the key findings? What do I *really* need to know? We've got a business to run!"

It seems like a year doesn't go by where there isn't some survey that points out that companies are investing more in analytics or "Big Data," but are still finding a big gap. Some point to the organization's lack of resource and/or know-how for data management, lack of focus, not hiring the proper analytical talent, or organizational structure as common roadblocks.

What's also common in these reports is that, for the companies that are seeing progress, there's always that prediction that the major gaps will

1

be closing in two to five years. When I see that same type of survey the following year, the results seem to be mostly the same, but once again, it will say things will improve over the next two to five years.

While some of the proposed solutions make a lot of sense in terms of how to fix the structure or improve the culture at a high-level, there is very little an analyst in the trenches can grab onto to help with their day-to-day struggles in supporting their internal clients with the key information they really need. There also seems to be a lot of focus on the latest analytic hot areas, from big data to machine learning to artificial intelligence.

While technological developments continue to improve, and understanding both analytic and data extraction techniques are important, what seems to be missing is how to navigate the interaction and communication between the analysts and the clients they support. If both parties are disconnected or not talking the same language, or both, no amount of structural planning or cool software can bridge that gap.

This book is focused on cleaning up that link that many times goes broken between analyst and client. It offers a way of working that will help the analyst focus more on being a successful analytical communicator, data translator, and ultimately the detective that gets the call when there's an important analytical case to solve.

CHAPTER 1

THE ANALYTIC
TRIFECTA

The latest data just came in, and the company Not Enough Inc. (NEI) is seeing a slowdown in sales volume for its top product.[1] Folks are concerned and want answers. As the company's marketing team, sales head, and product analyst file into the conference room, there's that general sinking feeling this is going to be an intense start to the week.

As they get started, the team leader opens by saying, "Hope everyone had a good weekend. We just received another data point this morning and we continue to see a slowdown in sales. As we go through some of the slides with the updated information, I'm asking for some real answers about the key drivers of this downward trend, and suggestions for actions we can take to move things back in the right direction."

The marketing department steps up to present their slides.

---

1 Not Enough Inc. (NEI) is a fictional company, and any similarity to an existing company is coincidental.

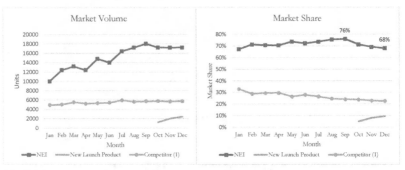

Figure 1.1

"As you can see, our sales volume continues to remain flat this month, and our new competitor is having a pretty decent launch of their new product," the head of marketing says.

The team leader looks around and takes note of the mixed concentration. Looking a little annoyed he points out, "I understand that when a competitor's new product launches they are going to get some of our business, and it's not uncommon for our share to slow up a bit, but the drop is more than I expected. Why do you think that's happening?"

At this point the team leader looks around the room making eye contact quickly with each person in the room.

"We heard our competitor has put a fair amount of resourcing against this launch, as well as providing a large number of free samples to our top customers across the country," the marketing head says.

"That's standard practice for new product launches, so I'm still not understanding the drop," the team leader says.

"Agreed," the marketing head says. "We are going through the different usual suspects to see if any patterns arise. We first looked at our top-tier customers as well as our mid-tier customers to see if anything dramatic was happening there. When we look at those two groups nationally, we see similar patterns of slowdown, however, that slowdown is a little stronger among our top-tier customers."

A slide goes up that shows the top and mid-tier customer lines, with the top-tier line slowing down more than the mid-tier line.

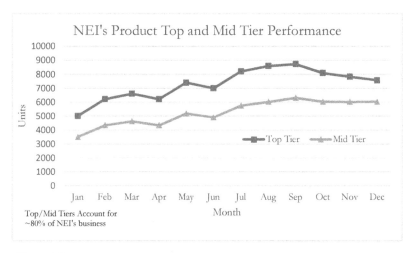

Figure 1.2

"Why do you think this might be happening?" the team leader asks.

"Usually, when new products launch, the early adopters of those products are in the top-tier."

"Okay. Can you pull together a list of those customers, so we can take a look at them?"

The marketing lead looks over at the analytics person to get quick visual confirmation that they're not going to promise something that can't be delivered. Head is nodding.

"Sure. We can pull that list together after the meeting."

"And what about patterns? Are we seeing any patterns across our SKUs?"

"Not really. When we look across our different SKUs, we once again see similar slowdowns across each segment, so nothing is really showing up there."

• • •

The last slide that goes up is a cut-and-paste from a field report that's a bit hard to read.

| NEI Product Units | Months | | | | | | Growth | Growth | Percent of |
Regions	July	Aug	Sep	Oct	Nov	Dec	Recent Month	Rolling Qtr.	Business
Northeast	4,428	4,644	4,878	4,681	4,678	4,680	0.0%	0.6%	27%
Northwest	2,460	2,580	2,736	2,633	2,640	2,632	(0.3%)	1.7%	15%
Midwest	1,640	1,720	1,836	1,790	1,789	1,807	1.0%	3.6%	11%
Central	1,968	2,064	2,178	2,100	2,116	2,133	0.8%	2.2%	12%
West	4,100	4,300	4,410	4,130	4,042	3,957	(2.1%)	(5.3%)	23%
Southeast	1,804	1,892	1,962	1,876	1,935	1,996	3.1%	2.6%	12%

Figure 1.3

The team leader walks right to the screen to see it better.

The team leader asks, "Is there something happening in the West region?

The sales head says, "I'm hearing some recent rumblings from the Southwest portion of that region, but they're not completely sure what's going on. We've also had some turnover in that area. I will speak with the regional sales manager to get an update right after this meeting.

The team leader says, "As I mentioned at the outset, I need some real answers about the key drivers of this downward trend. I'd like you to dig into where you see the most dramatic movement and why. I'm open to any theories, but want those theories substantiated with good analytics. It's all-hands-on-deck, so go to it. Let's turn this around."

• • •

This type of meeting is common in most industries. There appear to be a couple of clues in the data (e.g., some movement in top customers, declines in the Southwest), but they need to be pulled together and connected somehow by the analyst.

ABOUT ME

A little bit about who I am: I originally studied applied math and statistics as an undergraduate at Stony Brook University, as well as computer science. In my senior year, I found out that statistics was a lot more interesting than what was portrayed in the textbooks. I went on to graduate school at University of Connecticut (UConn), where I got my PhD in statistics.

During my last few years at UConn, I also got to teach introductory and advanced statistics classes as a lecturer in the statistics department.

From there I went out into the business world and have spent the last 34 years in what has been commonly referred to today as data science or analytics. Early in my career I did a lot of statistical model building at Donnelley Marketing and then in financial services at American Express. From there I started a small company called The Marketing Investigators (aka TMI Associates), where I was exposed to analytical challenges in financial services, insurance, automotive, entertainment, and even legal consultation. In 2002, I started working in pharmaceutical analytics, and have remained there ever since.

While some of the analytical terminology has changed throughout the years, as well as the incredible improvement in technology, I've found that there are constants throughout my 34 years in the field that have not changed. In fact, some of the disconnects I've seen on the analytic front remain. I've found that much of these disconnects center around overall communications as well as the understanding of the analyst's role in the organization.

I hope with this book to shed some light on where the common disconnects occur between analysts and the clients they support, and why they happen. My goal is to help you bridge that communication gap, and provide some tools to get there. Those who do analytics will definitely recognize the situations I'm talking about, but may not have thought about why there sometimes is this quiet frustration between analyst and client.

While this book is geared more toward those starting in analytics, individuals who are more experienced in analytics can also benefit from it. The more experienced analysts may also find benefit in some of the scenarios I discuss and how they can be more effective in their analytic communication. My sincerest hope is that this book can help get anyone who loves analytics to not only get more exposure in their organization, but to also be a big part of the key decision-making as well.

WHAT DATA ANALYSTS DO

The analyst's job is challenging in many ways. They must answer data-related questions posed by those they support. This can be a marketing team, sales team, a specific functional team within the organization, or their own managers in the analytical group. They must possess the technical skills to navigate through all the different available data, which is usually spread across multiple files within an internal system or datamart, or may be located outside that system. Analysts must have a good working knowledge of each of the databases, where they're located, what they're called, and any special rules they must apply before working with them. For example, they may need to remember that the company's customer database has both active and inactive customers, and that most questions are around active customers. As a result, they must instinctively know to only select active customers when mining the data.

Once that's done, the analyst must piece together the information required, whether through matching, merging, selecting, or deleting records to begin analyzing the data. Once the data has been prepared, they must apply their analytical and reasoning skills to move through the actual analysis.

Some business acumen is also necessary to understand what types of results are not useful, and to avoid as much as possible, going down analytic rabbit holes that don't produce useful findings. Finally, once the analysis is complete, they must be able to clearly communicate the results, as well as be prepared to manage expectations when questions around their findings arise.

When pulling together data, good analytics deals with answering three basic questions:

1. What does the data show?
2. Why is it happening, or why is it important?
3. How are we as a team addressing it? How does this help the business?

These are essentially the whats, whys, and hows of analytics, and for the whole analytic effort to work, you need to hit what I like to call the Analytic Trifecta.

The interesting part about the Analytic Trifecta is that many individuals stop at one, the "what," and either feel that two, the "why," and three, the "how," are out of the scope of what they do, or they just don't know how to get past the "what."

THE "WHAT"

When getting started on the "what," the first step requires knowing where the information you need is located and the technical ability to manipulate that information (or have someone assist you with this). This will involve pulling all the attributes or variables you're interested in, potentially matching and merging different datasets, as well as knowing how to keep the records you want, and filtering out records you don't want. All this needs to be done before you can summarize the information.

This initial step can be a heavy lift. Databases don't typically present themselves in the manner that you would like to have them prepared. In fact, they can be very messy. There could be lots of missing data where you expected information, letters or codes where you expected numerical information, or two different formats in two different datasets for the same exact attribute. You could also be dealing with databases that have not been updated, or the information is simply not there. Sometimes the logic required to pull data can be challenging (e.g., pull all customers who joined any time over the last two years and time align each customer's consumption from their first month to their most recent month). This step can be quite daunting. As you become more experienced with the data environment, you'll know how to assess how time consuming this step will be.

The next step, once the data is prepared, is to summarize the data. For example, in the case of a marketing or sales analysis, this may entail looking at what's going on with sales over some period of time, what percent of business comes from different age or age/gender categories, or what are the sales volumes by state, year-to-date. For each of these examples, you want to look at the visuals associated with these different metrics. Where are the highs and lows? Are there any interesting trends? This summary step is a natural way to get a general picture of what is going on with your product and your competitors. This is sometimes referred to as looking at the descriptive statistics.

This "what" information is delivered in many forms. It may be delivered as a spreadsheet with multiple tabs, customized reports, or Power-Point slides where templates are then filled in with the latest numbers, or they may appear on some sort of dashboard.

THE "WHY"

When someone has a chance to take a look at this data, they first try to understand what it means, if it makes sense, and if there are there any pieces of information and/or trends where something unique is happening. Each individual reacts differently when data is presented to them. Based on each individual's objective and area of focus, they will hone in on certain portions of the analysis. However, the one thing in common that all consumers of data trends or interesting results share is to try to understand *why* certain things are happening. In other words, the minute the data is presented, and you find out information from the "what" phase, you immediately go to the "why" phase.

The "why" phase is probably the most difficult phase of the analysis. It requires an understanding in most cases outside the boundaries of the data itself. It requires an understanding of the business at a deeper level. In some companies this search for deeper meaning is called a deeper dive. As an analyst looking at the data, you won't always know the reasons why, however running these results by individuals who are more knowledgeable on the business side should help give you direction. You may have found something interesting, or just identified a pattern that is obvious to those who are in the know in that area. Either way you will get the benefit from this as an analyst as you will learn something about the business. "Why" exercises are truly the point of intersection where the data and analysis meet the business.

The "why" phase requires more skill than just putting data out on a spreadsheet or a dashboard. Analysts who get more involved with the "why" phase start to think very differently about the way data will ultimately need to be presented to the business. This is a good thing.

Good back-and-forth discussion between those involved with the business and the analyst during this "why" phase will lead in directions that will get much closer to actionable insights.

Usually, during this phase you are first digesting the data, asking why the pattern is there, and either knowing the answer or more commonly positing a theory as to why this may be happening. Assessing whether this theory holds water will most likely require another—hopefully quick—analysis. If the theory is backed up by the data, you have some type of insight. You may continue to go down even deeper into more why questions. "Why is this happening? Because X is happening? Why is X happening?"

This could be painful for the analyst, as they're in the position of trying to run multiple follow-up analyses, which can be time consuming. It's easy to ask the questions, it's another thing to try to answer those questions. However, this back-and-forth iterative process between analyst and requester is organic, and is what you want to have occur. It gets both parties thinking more deeply about the data.

Many analysts shy away from this phase, or they feel that their job stops at the edge of "what." I strongly encourage those doing analyses to push past the "what" phase and engage in the "why" exercise. You don't have to know all the answers, but you should actively search for them. Solicit feedback from those who might have a better understanding of the business, as you might have some interesting theories to test out with the data. If they pan out, you may have found something very helpful and you may create a nice bond with those individuals who may have had a theory that you ultimately substantiated.

In short, this deep analytic dive phase is really what the analytic detective's journey is all about, and can have a marvelous payoff.

THE "HOW"

Once you been able to determine the reason why a certain trend or pattern is occurring or why certain observations stand out, the next questions would be:

1. Is there value in this result? (Advertising in certain metro areas shows stronger sales growth versus rural areas.)
2. Is it obvious and not really insightful? (Active customers spend, inactive customers don't.)
3. Is it just nice-to-know? (Our customers are slightly taller on average than the general population. There are exceptions here, of course, where height may be relevant for a certain type of product.)

If there is value in the result then the next question is *how* can it be addressed in such a way that helps grow the business? If the "what" and "why" yield truly interesting results, we may have stumbled onto a valuable insight. Sharing this insight with the team can generate very fruitful discussions. Keep in mind that one person's insight is another person's been there, done that, didn't work. Either way the data is taking you somewhere and as you interpret the results with some expert guidance from those who know the business, you at the very least as an analyst, will learn something. In a best-case scenario, you may have found something that can make a meaningful contribution to the business.

the ANALYTIC TRIFECTA

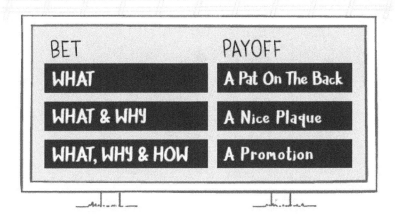

CHAPTER 2

ASSEMBLY REQUIRED

Before going into the analytic arena and putting on your analytic detective hat, you need to make sure you have all the software and access at your disposal to get the data, manipulate files, and have the procedures required available in the software you're using to analyze that data.

In general, I have found that questions you are asked by clients don't always align perfectly with the way internal databases are stored. Simply stated, information required will, more often than not, cut across multiple and separate databases. Additionally, there might be special programming required to align the data exactly the way you need it in order to start running a particular analysis.

For example, you might have a database on customers and their monthly purchases. The question posed might be something like, "On average, how much do customers purchase in their first six months as a new customer?" To answer this type of question you'll need, in most cases, some special programming up front to get the data set in the format so purchasing behavior is properly time-aligned. You may have a resource assigned to you that can pull data from the main databases based on your request and send it to you in the format you need so that you can do the analysis.

Another possibility is that there's an internal software tool you need to learn to get the data on your own. A third possibility is that you're knowledgeable in a more "popular" software package (or programming language) that your company purchases (or would support purchasing for downloading), and as a result you're able to extract the data on your own. This is especially useful when you're in a time crunch.

Personally, I'm a fan of the third possibility. While you don't have to know every nuance of a particular software package or programming language, you want to have the ability to get what you need and do the analysis on your own. Working on improving your skills using this software is very important. Try pulling together data using certain questions you may have encountered recently or create similar questions on your own. Figure out how you would pull that information together and see if your approach works. You may even save some of these procedures so you're not reinventing the wheel each time those type of requests come up.

Use your spare time to hone these skills. If you can't figure out how to do something, there may be an expert colleague who can help, there may be technical support for the specific software you're using, or you may even be able to find some answers online. In time, you will find that the request types are somewhat similar, and you will become more proficient pulling data together yourself when the need arises.

Throughout my career I have come in contact with a number of statistical software packages and have learned a few programming languages. What I have found is that for data analysis, Statistical Analysis System (SAS) software combined with learning Microsoft Excel—especially Microsoft Excel Pivot tables—has served me extremely well.

Having said that, I want to be clear that I'm not recommending any software packages as being the best. Whatever works well for you is what you should stick with, as long as those tools don't slow you down. In addition, based on the area that you work, certain software packages are going to make much more sense as the software of choice. You just want to make sure that you're not spending too much time trying to get data and massaging it into the form you need before you've even started an analysis.

In fact, a global study commissioned by the company Alteryx in 2019 found that, "Fifty-four million data workers worldwide spend 44 percent of their workday on unsuccessful data activities."[2]

"In general, I have found that questions you are asked by clients don't always align perfectly with the way internal databases are stored."

With respect to the popular data analytics software, there are always articles and surveys on the latest best list of products to choose from. Depending on who you talk to, you will find what constitutes their top products, as well as up-and-coming products. In some industries the debate rages between SAS, Python, and R. In the Burtch Works annual surveys you're seeing much more popularity these days around the open-sourced Python and R, though SAS is still a widely used tool within the data analytics industry.[3]

There are also many other popular products like Tableau, Microsoft Power BI, QilkView, Sisense, Apache Spark, Apache Storm, and or course Excel, to mention just a few.[4] These products show up year after year and offer some analytic software suggestions.

No matter what list you look at, you should not be dissuaded from using your favorite software package. Whatever package(s) you choose, try answering real questions posed by the business. Are you able to pull together

---

[2] "IDC Research Report: Taking Analysts' Time Back," Alteryx, April 2019, https://www.alteryx.com/research-study-third-party/idc-state-of-data-science-and-analytics.

[3] "2021 Survey: Python the Tool of Choice for Data Scientists & Analytics Pros." Burtch Works, August 3, 2021. https://www.burtchworks.com/2021/08/03/2021-survey-python-the-tool-of-choice-for-data-scientists-analytics-pros/.

[4] Gaurav Vohra, "25 Most Popular Data Analytics Tools to Know in 2021," Jigsaw Academy, March 8, 2021, https://www.jigsawacademy.com/10-most-popular-analytic-tools-in-business/.

that information easily, or do you find that while the software looks impressive, you need to bring in someone else to make big adjustments to the data to answer that one question? Does that happen often? If so, you're going to be in that 44 percent mentioned earlier. In addition, make sure that your product has good support, and take note of whether this software is used throughout your industry. You'll want to have this software knowledge as a transferrable skill, should you move to another company.

One summer I managed some interns who were interested in analytics. They all had familiarity with Microsoft Excel and could put together a spreadsheet, summarize data, work on some small datasets, and put together some graphs. I had them work on questions that were relevant to the business at that time, and they were very excited to be part of the action. I made sure they could play with data sets that didn't exceed the size of Excel. I also gave them some quick training on pivot tables.

Typically, when getting started on an analytic exercise, it is quite common to have to pull data from large databases of several million records. These databases will also have a large number of variables. If there are multiple large databases each housing the information required, then there will likely be a need to match, merge, and filter to get the analytic file in the shape you want to start the analysis. For example, one request might be to look at active customer's spending over the last six months by month. In addition, there might be an interest in looking at those customer's ages, genders, states, as well as some sort of behavioral (low, medium, high) segments. To accomplish this, you would need to work with active customer transactional data over the last six months in conjunction with some customer profile and customer segment type data.

What the interns realized was that it didn't take much to exceed the limits of Excel when they were looking to analyze larger datasets and answer business questions that came up every few days. At that point I showed them some simple SAS procedures to get at the bigger databases. I also showed them how to get some bigger databases downloaded for Excel pivoting. What they discovered is that with just a little coaching help, they could act somewhat independently and pull together data on their own, even when the requests were a little tricky.

The point of this is to illustrate that when analysts feel they can get to any of the databases they need using the software tools available to them, they can think more about the analytic problem itself rather than managing their analytic tools.

Consider a chef who is about to make a specific meal for you. Once you've placed your order, the chef has to pull all the items together to start preparing your meal. Imagine that the chef had to drive to various locations to get all the ingredients after the order was placed. At some locations the items are available. At other locations, the necessary items are available but they're in a bunch of different rooms, so they take more time to collect. Now the chef is driving back to the kitchen, and when he arrives, you're wondering how things are progressing. Your impression is that the food is being prepared, but in reality, that part of the process hasn't even started.

This situation is similar to what happens when a business poses a question to an analyst. The person posing the question is mostly unaware of all the work required just to pull everything together before any analysis begins. As an analyst, you want be cognizant of the types of questions that come your way and what type of information is typically asked for. This way you can have the tools at your disposal necessary to get the data and organize the information as best as you can. Of course, you can't always anticipate the questions, and for some situations you may have to start building from scratch. Take note of these situations and see if you can make adaptations when future questions of this type come in so you can design your approach to get to the analysis stage sooner. You don't want to be driving all around town, so to speak, trying to pull the information together.

As you become more entrenched with the analytic requests and hopefully deliver the results, make a study of what was asked. Is this something that will most likely come up often with a particular client or other clients, or is it more likely a one-time request? If this question type were to surface again, would you be able to reduce the time it takes to get to the analysis stage? For example, let's look again at the question mentioned earlier about what customers spend each month in their first six months as a new customer. Could I incorporate this time-aligned data into a database and other variables that the customer might be interested in, e.g., age, gender, etc., so that I'd have easy access? If you can organize the data in such a way that you can go right to the analysis, whether that analysis is basic or more advanced, you will think more about the analytics and less about the data preparation.

I've seen many analysts work hard on a particular analysis, spending a great deal of time on the data preparation stage, only to start from scratch again when the follow-up question had a slight variation from the original.

On the extreme side I have seen groups spend a great deal of time trying to set up databases that they believe will answer every type of question. These exercises can become all-consuming with folks trying to design data structures they believe will answer almost any question anyone might ask. This effort of trying to account for every eventuality usually doesn't work, especially when the business questions are more in-depth and layered. Additionally, many software presentations like to strut their stuff, showing what looks like a typical business question and how easy it is to show a whole bunch of ways to seamlessly answer those questions. With just one-click of a button all the graphs, charts, and maps you need are ready to go.

One software presentation I recall from a while back set up a hypothetical question where we would be looking for customers who were very active across the overall market, but had a low market share for our product. With a couple of clicks you could select these specific customers by selecting the criteria you wanted. This was easily executed with the software using drop-downs. Once this was done, a map was pulled up and you could see the distribution of these select customers throughout the US. You then could pick any part of the map and zoom in or zoom out. Zooming in you could see more defined clusters of these customers. If you hovered over any one of these customer data points, you would see all the different information about this individual.

I remember folks being very impressed at the time—they loved the maps. Doing analytics seemed so simple. As impressive as this was and many software products today can do this, the reality is that answering many of the day-to-day questions is usually not as straightforward. It's hard to predict in advance many of the questions that will be asked of you. As a result, the software demo environment is not always representative of the real environment. In most situations, there is some data preparation work that has to be done once the question is posed.

There are going to be many questions that will be asked in which the raw data can be accessed from the company database. In order to answer those questions, you cannot always jump right to the answer without putting together the data. It may be simple or may be more complex, but either way there is always some assembly required.

As an analyst, you want to minimize the time it takes from the ask to the analysis. Learn from each experience, make a conscious study on the question patterns, and ask yourself if you can make your up-front process more efficient. Doing so will get you to the detective phase much sooner.

CHAPTER 3

AD-HOC:
MEATBALL SURGERY

W hen I came out of graduate school, I wanted to use a lot of the different statistical techniques I had learned and apply them to the various problems and challenges the business was facing. I had this vision that I would be building models of all kinds that would predict different types of customer or prospect behavior and I would get to see how well those models performed when deployed. I was also interested in automating certain processes that were often asked for so that I could turn things around quickly and at the same time keep internal clients happy. Early in my career I got to do a lot of this type of modeling and automation. That feeling of "this is really cool" drove me. Building a model that actually could generate results for the business was always exciting.

However, the more common day-to-day demand, especially in this current fast-paced environment, is to get quick answers to questions related to what's going on with the business at that particular point in time. Questions may entail pulling numbers like counts, percents, or growth rates. Sometimes analysts feel that "running numbers" is a little beneath them. They've been academically trained to do much more sophisticated work, and they want to apply those skills. But many clients like to digest the data and think through what's happening with the business in this manner. They even commit the key numbers to memory, and believe that analytic folks are doing the same. Analysts are generally more interested in the patterns behind those numbers. This is of course just as important.

Einstein, according to the story, was once asked by a colleague for his phone number. Einstein went right to the phone book to look it up. The colleague was surprised that Einstein didn't know his own phone number, to which Einstein responded, "Never memorize something that you can look up." He felt that your brain should not be cluttered with information that is easily retrievable.[5]

For someone who has a degree in analytics, they tend to feel the same way about memorizing population sizes, growth rates, market shares, or percent of business for key segments. Usually the higher the academic degree, the less interest in memorization. However, if you want your clients to trust you, you may need to either risk the brain clutter and become familiar with some of the key business numbers or find a way to retrieve them very quickly when asked. Keep in mind that a good detective is always searching for patterns and explanations, but at the same time they're always grounded and very knowledgeable of the basic facts.

I have seen two types of analytic requests: the first are the quick turn-around analytics that I just described, and the other is the need for longer-term analytics. The longer-term analytics usually entails either building some type of model and/or initiating some large data mining exercise to answer a big question, such as:

- What is the profile of our different customers?
- Do they fall into distinct groups or segments?
- What is the Return on Investment (ROI) for each of these groups?
- How do we optimize a particular effort?

These examples are typically considered advanced analytics.

The shorter-term analytics that require quick turnaround are usually not couched as big analytic projects, but more about pulling information related in some way to some customer or prospect segments. They could be

---

[5] Gail Saltz, *The Power of Different: The Link Between Disorder and Genius* (New York: Flatiron Books, 2017), 56.

a "how many are there" request and/or "how are they performing" against certain metrics request.

Some companies may carve out a group that focuses on just the advanced analytics, working on longer-term projects, and have another group work on the short-term requests. There are pros and cons to working in these separate groups. I've found that the longer-term projects can be very exciting but are typically less client-facing day-to-day. There is also a danger that due to the urgency to get answers, the long-term requests can trail off in importance.

The short-term requests are usually more client facing and are more unpredictable. Analysts here need to be keenly aware of the different resources and databases available. They also need to develop more speed in pulling things together and producing some quick results. While this activity can be much more pressurized and seem haphazard, you are much closer to how individuals are thinking about the business in real time.

What's interesting is that the short- and long-term efforts are both looking to discover important patterns in the data to help inform the business how to move forward, where to invest effort, where things are working, and where they're not.

When working with most internal clients, as I mentioned earlier, their day-to-day is trying to answer questions about the business and what to do about it ASAP. You may hear the term ad-hoc analysis bandied about. Ad-hoc analyses are essentially analytic requests that emerge that particular day or week. They are usually born from a specific question or problem that people don't know the answer to and believe can be answered by pulling and analyzing information from internal databases. Other types of ad-hoc requests arise from examining why something went wrong in an analytic process or resolving why certain numbers don't match up. In short, the term ad-hoc is fairly wide ranging.

There is generally no way to know when these ad-hoc requests are going to happen and how time consuming or difficult they will be to answer. Ad-hoc requests are going to come your way and will divert your attention from a pre-planned (possibly longer-term) analysis or effort you might be working on. These newly arriving ad-hoc requests will also most likely jump to top priority status.

Ad-hoc requests by their nature are very unpredictable. They can come from a reaction to some business dynamic that's occurring, a "what if" scenario question, or even investigating reasons around some sort of data disconnect issue, to mention only a few. Here are some examples:

1. Business is slowing down in certain areas of the country. I need reports on our different customer segments. I want to look at specific metrics that might be different than what's in the standard reports. For example, what's our weekly promotional effort in these areas?
2. What if we focused more effort in certain areas? What number of prospects would there be? What is their potential?
3. What do two different reporting systems that are supposedly tracking the same thing show? Why are there differences?

It should also be mentioned that many ad-hoc requests usually generate more ad-hoc requests once they are answered (part of the "what" and "why" iteration mentioned in Chapter 1).

There is a tendency to try to avoid this unpredictable ad-hoc environment as an analyst, and many analysts do. It is a much faster paced environment, can be very stressful, and in many cases, you may not feel you have the necessary time to get the work done. When presented with these questions, think about why they're asking that particular question. If you can get a better understanding of the rationale, you can do a better job with your answers. You may even know the follow-up questions instinctively, and you can incorporate into your analysis as you start to see the initial results. Once you start thinking this way, you're actually being a more proactive analyst. I write more about this in Chapter 7.

I've generally found that this type of proactive involvement gets you closer to what folks are thinking about to move the business. If you get good at this, and you can give good direction from what you're finding, folks will begin to appreciate that you're really helping them get their questions answered. You may even experience that, in time, you'll have a seat at the table where the real action and decision-making happens, and you're a part of it. I've seen this evolution of first just "running numbers," to being asked "What do you think?" to seeing these individuals being asked to join an important leadership meeting, as they are considered very knowledgeable about the patterns in the data. They're usually dumbfounded and a little scared that they're being invited, but they're also excited that their efforts are being recognized, just from this invitation. Ideally, if you can get exposure to both short-term and longer-term analytic work, you will get a better understanding of how each area works.

It's always a good idea to remember that no one has all the answers and that those who are making requests don't always know what they're going to find. They may be trying to work through some theories on their end that may not make sense to you, and may not ultimately bear fruit. Often, they're not exactly sure what the story might be. When they get the results, they might go down a different path. Either way, this is typically how the ad-hoc world works. It is a process that doesn't always go straight from A to B.

Sometimes analysts think that all questions that can be answered from data already in-house should be asked precisely in advance, and in such a way that they can time everything out and come back with a time/cost estimate of how long it's going to take—even going so far as getting a sign-off on the request. Usually in the ad-hoc world, hearing a long timeline, not to mention a sign-off, is very frustrating to the requester. However, in some specific cases it might be warranted.

If you show that you can turn certain things around quickly and that you're not the type of person who immediately puts up a roadblock when a question is asked, you'll get a lot more traction and understanding with something that takes more time (possibly due to the complexity of the request, or challenges getting data).

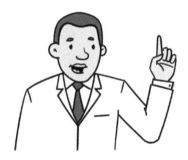

"You may even experience that, in time, you'll have a seat at the table where the real action and decision-making happens, and you're a part of it."

One of the most popular shows of the 1970s, *M*A*S*H*, had a term the surgeons used to categorize the type of fast-paced surgery they had to perform under the incredibly adverse conditions of war.

They called it "meatball surgery." The idea was to stabilize the patients quickly and move to the next one. Major Charles Emerson Winchester, a newly-arriving advanced surgeon, liked to move methodically, and famously said, "I do one thing at a time, I do it very well, and then, I move on."[6]

The other surgeons told him that you need to "patch-'em up and get-'em out." Winchester felt this approach was rather "primitive," and said, "Short cuts are sloppy surgery." The surgeons showed him that faster methods worked just as well, without compromising safety, and that they've gotten very efficient by "sheer repetition." Not every procedure can be rushed through, and indeed Winchester performs a complicated advanced successful surgery during a less busy time, which the other surgeons were not familiar with. Ultimately, Winchester realizes that he has to be able to move at the other surgeon's pace, and in time he gets the hang of things.

I sometimes think of the ad-hoc world as "meatball surgery." You can be effective and get to good results in many situations, without turning every request into a large project.

Short-term ad-hoc work is usually not sexy and you can feel like it's beneath you to do, but keep in mind that it can lead you and your clients to some interesting insights. Even the best detectives have had to rummage or even dive into some dumpsters to get some critical clues.

In short, if you can manage the short-term well, you will start thinking much faster on your feet, not to mention become more familiar with all the different databases and resources in the company. You might even get a better understanding of the different facets of the business. In time you may manage a group of analysts who can do this work. Most importantly, you will become a valued analytic asset in the organization.

---

[6] *M*A*S*H*, season 6, episode 1, "Fade Out, Fade In," directed by Hy Averback, written by James Fritzell and Everett Greenbaum, aired September 20, 1977, CBS.

CHAPTER 4

GOT DATA?

As the famous statistician William Edwards Deming once said, "Without data you're just another person with an opinion."[7] And everyone has one.

As analysts we are clearly dependent on data and the ability to access that data.

Companies spend a lot of money on data. There are many different sources of data. Internal transactional data, information about individuals that are part of your customer base, as well as data about potential prospects for your products are all sources of data companies tend to compile. There is also data that is relevant and compiled by outside vendors who can then sell this data to you. That data can then be transferred to the company database. Additionally, there is data available from website activity as well as social media activity.

The focus here will be on data that resides within the company systems in some standard database format. This type of data is usually referred to as structured data (as opposed to unstructured data, such as streaming audio, video, weblogs, and social media).

---

[7] Milo Jones and Philippe Silberzahn, "Without an Opinion, You're Just Another Person with Data," *Forbes*, March 15, 2016, https://www.forbes.com/sites/silberzahnjones/2016/03/15/without-an-opinion-youre-just-another-person-with-data/?sh=7364b198699f.

Becoming familiar with all the potential databases you can interact with is essential to doing good quality analysis. That may sound simple, but given the vastness of all these different databases and all the information that's compiled, becoming an expert on all the individual pieces of information residing in the company database is quite challenging. Conversely, not understanding the information extremely well can also really screw up your analysis.

Unfortunately, data dictionaries in many cases don't go into too much detail about what a variable means, how it was compiled, or any warnings about missing data or general misuse of the data. Sometimes, there's no data dictionary at all, and you either have to make assumptions about what certain variables mean, or find someone who might be in the know about that data (assuming they are still with the company).

As an analyst, you're usually left to your own devices to kick around the different pieces of information on the database and get familiar with the formats. You also have to get a sixth sense about what looks like a minefield in the data. I liken this experience to going into someone's garage and seeing the different things they have, what's in each of the boxes, what shape are they in, and so on. As I'm not familiar with how they've organized everything, I have to become familiar with what's available, what works and what might not work so well. In truth, I feel that way in my own garage when I'm looking for something I haven't looked for in a while. Either way, if I don't really look around and "kick the tires" so to speak, I might miss something important, or misuse something and possibly get hurt, because I didn't carefully check it out in advance.

Many years ago, when I was new to the analytic group at my company, the marketing team was concerned that overall product sales were not meeting forecast expectations and had some concern that sales representative effort had slowed down. (Sales representatives typically have a list of customers and/or prospects that they call on.) When I pulled the weekly sales call activity data, I noticed that indeed the last two weeks had dropped significantly. I quickly charted the trend so you could see the drop in activity. I showed this chart to the brand director and he immediately asked me to throw this in a slide. During a weekly brand update with senior marketing and sales leadership, my slide went up. This slide was the flashpoint of this meeting. The sales leadership was miffed as to why the last two weeks were soft, but promised to address the issue with the field.

Later that day I was having a conversation with someone who knew this data a bit better than I did. I mentioned the two-week softness. He then told me, "Oh, the last two weeks are never complete, as the system doesn't completely synch the call files." The bottom line is that it's always a good idea to carefully check out and understand what's in the company's "data garage."

Another example that has stuck with me from a long time ago was a model profile that was built on prospects who responded to a particular product offer in a direct mail campaign. Typically, in a direct mail campaign you have the list of individuals that were sent mail, and after the mailing is complete, you have, for each individual, whether they responded or not. You then attach as much information that you have available in your database about each individual, and look for discernable patterns between the responders and non-responders that can be used to predict the behavior of newly available prospects. Fortunately, there was an internal prospect database that had a lot of different pieces of information (variables) about all the individuals who were mailed (e.g., age, gender, average home value, individual's length of residence, etc.).

The modeling work that was done looked at different groups of variables that correlated well with the responsiveness of the individuals mailed. The final model profile variables were either positively correlated with responsiveness or negatively correlated with responsiveness. Positively correlated means that higher values of that variable tracked with higher responsiveness, and lower values of that variable tended to track with lower responsiveness. Negatively correlated means just the opposite: that higher values of that variable tended to track with lower responsiveness, and lower values of that variable tended to track with higher responsiveness.

One of the variables that drove the model was the number of cars owned by the household. The correlation was positive, i.e., the more cars you owned the more likely you were to have responded to the offer. The presenter highlighted this result, and a lot of discussion focused around trying to understand why folks with more cars liked the offer. Was this just a proxy for wealthier customers? This seemed odd because the previous experience with this particular offer was that responders tended to reside in mid- to lower-average income areas where you would expect fewer cars per household. When asked about the average number of cars that were observed on responders, the average number was five to six cars. This seemed very unusual. The average prospect owned five to six cars? Upon further inspection, the distribution of cars for responders was something like:

Number of Cars	Number of Reponders	Percent of Responders	Total Mailed	Response Rate
1	1,500	24%	103,448	1.45%
2	1,000	16%	90,909	1.10%
3	500	8%	56,180	0.89%
9	3,300	52%	86,614	3.81%

Figure 4.1

The immediate question was why were there so many people with nine cars. Was that correct? Looking closer, it was revealed that the value "9" was put in this field when the number of cars was unknown. In fact, "9" was simply missing data.

The result did not have to do with increased car ownership, but simply that prospects where there was information about cars available were less responsive than those where that information was not available. The takeaway had more to do with whether those prospects appeared on compiled lists (i.e., info was available) and were probably contacted a lot more previously versus those who didn't show up on compiled lists (i.e., info was not available), and were not contacted as often.

The example illustrates that even though the data was processed correctly for the model, the extreme value of "9," which made up over half of the responders (52 percent), ended up having an impact on the final result and created an incorrect interpretation.

Another example that comes up often is where you find what appears to be a fascinating relationship or correlation that looks too good to be true. As the saying goes, it probably is. In a fictional analysis I ran, the software found a strong correlation between spending and an individual's status. This individual's status variable has four codes ("P," "A,""I," "N"). The query I ran shows that status "A" is where all the current spending is. The software essentially found a perfect predictor for spending. When this happens you've probably found something that is painfully obvious, and not checking it out thoroughly will generate a different type of PAIN should you actually present this without checking further. In this case, the data dictionary wasn't available, but more digging indicated that "P" is a Prospect, "A" is an active customer, "I" means an inactive customer, and "N" is a non-customer who has yet to show interest in the product. So, the finding is that active customers spend on our product, non-customers and inactive customers do not spend on our product. Back in the data-mining days this used to be called "fool's gold." Essentially it has no value.

A similar situation akin to the "9s" example occurs when you see spikes in the data. These spikes are clear visual outliers, and when presented graphically really stand out. In fact, these spikes become the sole focus of the visual, as they are very hard for the eye to ignore. They essentially dwarf any other patterns that are present in the data. Are they correct? Do they make sense? What is a given is that they require more serious investigation.

When the data is very positive and would reflect well on them, I've seen folks try really hard to justify that those results must make sense. However, if the results look unusually negative, they immediately believe something must be wrong. An example would be a situation where sales have been pretty stable over the last 12 months, and then all of a sudden, they doubled in just one month. Compare this to sales being stable for 12 months and then halved in just one month. In either case, no matter how emotionally attached you are to the results, the analyst must dig deeper and find out what's happening. The results may be justified based on certain extreme conditions, but they must still be checked, good or bad.

My experience is that dramatic outliers usually have a rational explanation. In many cases the underlying causes are either from some sort of process change, a change in some condition or method of counting, a process interruption, or an asymmetric update to a process where one end is updated and the other portion is not, or another type of apples-to-oranges comparison. No matter what the cause, it has to be analyzed and investigated thoroughly. If indeed the outlier explanation is due to some artificial condition or event that occurred, it needs to be called out and explained.

The reason I point out data examples like these is that your software package is going to go where the data leads it. It doesn't know whether relationships are obvious, something in a process changed, or the comparisons are not apples-to-apples. You, as an analyst, need to know what may be of value, what to ignore, and/or possibly standardize. Even so-called artificial intelligence (AI) software doesn't know what's obvious and what's not. It's just looking for patterns and/or strong correlations.

Beyond the obvious, I've seen some analysts stop when they don't understand what something means, but will tell me that's what the data says. That's not good enough. You as an analytic detective need to know that what you're finding has not only been processed correctly, but makes sense. If it doesn't, you need to dig in and find out why. If you have a legitimate result that seems counterintuitive, you need to understand what might be going on. It's possible there's something there that folks weren't aware of that might be helpful to understand. It may even be insightful and worth digging into. Either way, while you didn't compile the original raw data, you will need to deal with the data hand you're dealt and some-how make sense and/or salvage what can be gleaned from the data.

There is this impression to those requesting analyses that once the data has arrived, it's just a simple exercise to run the analysis. They have no idea that there are a whole bunch of data parts that arrive with no directions. It's even worse when variables appear to be something they're not, either because the definition is completely disconnected from what you expected, or there is such a large amount of missing data in the field itself. The "9 cars" example is a common missing data tale. When you mention something like 50 percent of the records having missing values to the person who requested that analysis, they can't believe it. They will insist that something must be wrong with the data. Imagine multiplying that disbelief for variables you have yet to decode. While there may be ways to improve the coverage of certain variables, the analysis clock is ticking and you have to do your best to manage this uncertainty.

As an analyst, you want to make sure you connect with folks who might be more familiar with the variables themselves and/or can help you find some way to the data source provider. Ideally, I have always advocated for having an information management role. This role would be in charge of making sure data flows on time, there is quality control on counts going in and going out, and can track down detailed data issues and/or disconnects. This role is a critical behind-the-scenes role that keep things on track. Unfortunately, many companies take this for granted. The role also helps analytics teams that don't want to be bogged down chasing what a variable means or why its coverage is lower than expected. Additionally, folks focused on the data quality can essentially deem the final data sets trusted sources. Anyone deriving different counts or percents will have to compare to the trusted source counts and percents to better understand why their numbers are different.

"You as an analytic detective need to know that what you're finding has not only been processed correctly, but makes sense."

The information management role is not to be confused with an information technology role, which deals more with the technology (design, processing) behind the databases, and not as much with the details of what is housed within each variable. There are some exceptions within IT departments, but an analyst wants to know a lot more detail about the data itself, especially when they are the ones presenting it.

One final note: in addition to becoming familiar with the different data sources available, you should always do what I call spot checks with those you're working with. What I mean by this is that you should compile some simple descriptive statistics on your own from the database that folks are familiar with. These can be things like total active customers, number of field targets, response rates, growth rates, or size of specific popular segments. Once you've run some of these numbers, you should informally pass them by people who would most likely know the results and make sure you're getting the same numbers. If they match, that's great. However, if they don't, you'll want to know if you've made some mistake or misinterpreted how to run that query. Better to find out early as opposed to finding out later after you put in an entire analytic effort.

Clearly a big part of the analytic detective's job is to have a good working knowledge of the data, an ability to access it, and a determination to closely examine findings on variables that seem important in order to make sure there's nothing that would raise question. You always have to ask the question, "Do the results make sense?" Remember, understanding the (trusted) data well will give you the edge over opinion almost every time.

CHAPTER 5

GOING FROM REQUEST TAKER TO COLLABORATOR

So now you've got your favorite software package set up, you've figured out how to link to all the key databases, and you're becoming more familiar with the data itself. You're ready to dig in. What's your next move?

Well, who are your clients? Remember, analytics is a support function. You are there to help individuals, using your analytic skills, try to figure out how to "crack the code" to best move the business forward. These clients may be in marketing, sales, or some other function that is in a decision-making position for the business. You may also need to field questions from leadership in your own analytic group. At any given time, you could be juggling questions from a number of different client types, each with different styles and needs.

One prerequisite is that you know who your key clients are. Key clients are the ones who are paying the bills for your support. These clients can be internal and/or external. You want to make sure you understand that up-front. If you're not sure, you need to have that "who are my main clients" conversation with your boss. This is not to say that you won't try to help out others if you can, but your job is to support specific clients. (As a side note, but an important one, make sure to add your boss and leaders in your organization as key clients as well.)

When you're first connecting with each of these clients, use the meetings as an opportunity to gain an understanding of their position in the organization—what they're tasked with and what the most important questions they're trying to answer are. The more specific your client is, the better off you'll be. Getting an answer like, "I'm just trying to grow the business" is not specific. Ask them for some examples in their area. Every client I've met with is always more than happy to tell me what they work on and how I can help them.

When you have these meetings, bring a pad and *write things down*. Even if you have a great memory, write it down. Writing things down when you're meeting with people shows you want to get it right. In addition to good eye contact, it conveys that you're totally engaged. This is a good general rule that transcends just meetings about analytics.

You can be a great analyst, but if you don't take notes when a client has several questions, the client tends to think you aren't going to get to everything they need. Even if you did catch everything, it makes a stronger impression that you're taking the time to write it down. This can be even more important if a client asks you to confirm what you're going to take a look at ("playback"). If you missed something they deemed important, they will have to go over it again. It's simple: write it down or type it out somewhere (pad, laptop, iPad, etc.).

For each of those requests, your reaction as an analyst will be to figure out if raw data is available to answer it, then see how easy is it to compile, and lastly, think about how you're going to execute and summarize the actual analysis. As you start to go through this process in your head, you'll get an understanding of what you can pull together quickly, what may be more time-consuming, and what you might not be able to pull together at all.

As mentioned previously, it's important to continue to improve your software, database linkage, and data elements knowledge. Your client's requests will definitely put that knowledge to the test. In time you'll begin to discover that there are never "too many flavors" when it comes to the type of requests you get, and you'll spend less time thinking about the data compilation and more time thinking about the analytical execution and results delivery portion of the request.

Whichever portion of the request we're talking about, think about refining the types of skills you feel can have the greatest impact to your own process. For example, I used my downtime to build what I like to call "the kitchen sink" database. This had all the variables that were typically used in requests I received. However, I would make sure I could house it in a large easily updated Microsoft Access file locally, where I could pivot in Microsoft Excel or Power BI. I found this type of exercise made the most impact to my overall analytic process and thinking as I continued to refine this specific database.

As you become more familiar with the different clients you're working with, you should take note of what they usually ask. Sometimes analysts get so caught up in the mode of just taking requests and turning them around that they don't think much about how their clients are really thinking. There is also a tendency as an analyst to make the job only about request turnaround so you can finish the job. While this is a good feeling, you'll get a lot more out of the experience, and will make a stronger impact on your client, if you try to understand more about what they're really looking for.

"The bottom line is that, as an analyst, you need to go beyond just thinking about taking and fulfilling requests."

Here are some of examples of different client types. I will use the word "client" when referring to people the analyst is supporting and "customers" as people who are consumers of the company product.

1. ACQUISITION-FOCUSED CLIENTS

These types of clients are always thinking about how to bring in new business. They are generally looking for ways to attract new customers by understanding what got them started in the first place. They want to find new sources of data and see if they can extract key patterns. New sources of data could be information that is part of your data warehouse but not looked at very often, or could come from sources that aren't in-house. As an analyst, this might be exciting, but it is also very open-ended data mining work with no clear direction. You can go down a certain path and arrive at a dead end. The good news is when you do find something, it can lead to very interesting and potentially new conversations. Clients may look to you for ideas. This type of exercise needs to be done carefully, as you can start by pulling recent new customers, but you will also need to pull their information prior to the event of them becoming a new customer. From there you can look for patterns. This is detective work where you're looking for clues and there might not necessarily be a clear trail to follow.

For example, a client was interested in looking at the newest customers of their product, which had been on the market for a few years, and who joined the customer base over the last six months. They wanted to know if there was anything specific that differentiated them from the average customers. In addition, what information was available prior to them becoming customers that could have been used to potentially attract other prospects? Were these customers more responsive to certain messages? Were there offers of free product that got them hooked? In addition to information on these individuals housed internally, could we consider looking at data that could be purchased through a third-party data provider?

One of the quick analyses I was able to do is to look at some of the different variables on the internal database (age, gender, demographic, behavioral, contact history, offer types) and see if there were some stark differences between the new customer and older customer group. This is usually a good start to see what comes up and whether there is something there. In this particular example we saw bigger difference in free offer response and age. The data showed that new customers were more responsive to free offers than regular customers. It also showed that new customers skewed younger.

One important question to consider when analyzing or profiling likely new customers who might be responsive to a particular effort or fit a certain profile, is determining whether these prospects will become valued customers. There are many situations where you can acquire new customers, but based on certain information they are going to be unprofitable.

One example is making an offer of credit to an individual who is known to have an extremely poor credit rating. They will be happy to accept the offer and become a customer, but will also not pay their bills. There are other examples of prospects who know how to work the system and get the free offers for as long as they can, and then cancel just before they have to pay for something. This is sometimes referred to as churn, and it can have a very detrimental impact on the business.

As an analyst, you will need to bring a flexible mindset with this type of client as they are looking for unique ways to bring in new customers, and almost every variable is in play. However, you as analyst will also need to do your best to keep them focused so you can at some point narrow the scope to actionable findings, once they've been uncovered.

2. RETENTION-FOCUSED CLIENTS

Clients wired around retention are interested in taking care of the customers who keep the company going every day. For this reason, they want to keep a close eye on patterns that may indicate potential red flags that they are losing core customers. Customers whose activity levels have declined steadily or dramatically, have become inactive, or have voluntarily left your customer base, are the groups the retention-focused client wants to know about. They want to track these groups closely and get alerts if troublesome patterns start to emerge. It is quite common for these types of clients to want updated lists of potential "at-risk" customers so that they can find ways to take action and/or preempt an unwanted decline in customer activity.

For example, your client is interested in looking at top customers who have recently shown a large decline in purchasing. Depending on the industry, I've heard terms like "decliner analysis" or "anti-attrition analysis," where the latter are cases where the customer leaves the customer base. Who are these customers? Why are they declining? What can we do about it?

Pulling these "decliners," as well as an opposite group of "growers," and looking for differences across all the variable information about these individuals in each group, might get you started on where the problem might be occurring. Are there geographic dynamics? Is there a lower promotional effort of some sort in the decliner group?

There may also be customers who dramatically decline over a short period of time. Customers like these usually have had some type of event occur. It could have been a personal event or they could have had a poor customer service or product experience. Following up on these cases usually tend to prove very informative.

Understanding when and why these declining patterns occur and being able to do something positive about it as soon as possible is critical. I've found that for these types of clients finding ways to automate early detection can be challenging, exciting, and what your client is looking for.

3. FINANCIALLY FOCUSED CLIENTS

Clients of this type are keenly interested in whether a particular effort is cost effective. They like to track metrics like the cost-per-contact, revenue generated per customer, or lifetime value (LTV) of particular customers. Ultimately, they want to summarize specific tactics and/or strategies in terms of whether they have a good ROI. This can be very challenging as you may not have all the necessary information to make a precise call on ROI, and clearly knowing whether an ROI is positive has a lot of implications in terms of whether these efforts get reduced or increased funding. I will talk more about ROI, and some of the extra challenges that come with it in Chapter 13.

Clients like these are thinking very big picture. They will want to know the costs involved with certain efforts, as well as the lifetime value return of these customer segments. They like to make very high-level calculations, and can tell you rather quickly whether an effort is going to pay off. They usually like to consume the results in tabular form with cost of effort and/or tactic and some sort of return, either in totality or by year.

For those financially oriented clients for whom you are doing analytics, you should also become familiar with the general costs of particular efforts, net revenue of customers, how lifetime value is calculated, and how they vary across different segments.

4. DETAILED DATA-FOCUSED CLIENTS

These individuals want you to pull all the data for them so they can play with it on their own and perform their own brand of analytics. The most common transactions between analyst and detailed data focused clients are either via Microsoft Excel spreadsheets (potentially with multiple tabs) and/or Microsoft Access databases. Depending on the particular request, this could be either a good thing or bad thing for you as an analyst. On the one hand, these clients may lighten your load as they're doing a lot of the data summaries they need themselves; on the other hand they could create a problem for you if they misinterpret the data and send those results over the fence, unchecked. When this occurs, you are put in the precarious position of letting them know what they sent out is not correct. Additionally, these individuals could drain a lot of your time just pulling all sorts of different datasets that, had you known what they were trying to do, you could have done in far less time.

Personally, I've had a number of clients who like experimenting with the raw data, most of them in spreadsheet form. This is usually not too much of a problem to provide. At some point I will usually get to see how they're using the data. At that point, if I believe I can help them out based on how they're looking at the data, I will make a suggestion on a better way to proceed. Certain clients, while they appreciate the suggestion, like doing the data analysis on their own. As the analyst, you have to let them work through the data to get to their conclusions. Others really appreciate the simplification and may not need the detailed data, once you've been able to hone in on what they're really looking for.

In either case, a lot depends on the particular requests, but as their analytic support, you want to do your best to keep a close eye on what they're trying to accomplish, and ideally remain active in analytic guidance.

5. SUMMARY DATA-FOCUSED CLIENTS

Clients that are summary data–focused also like data, but the detail they're looking for is usually in some summarized form, like customized reports. They also want those reports to be formatted nicely and easy to read. Usually, they like getting this information in Excel, PowerPoint, and/or as a PDF. These clients like to cherry-pick key stats from these reports to convey what they're seeing with the business as well as supporting some theory that they have about a particular trend or pattern. Given that these clients are very directive about how they want to see the data I've generally found that it's best to directly accommodate their report requests. You can make suggestions, but if they stick to their guns, don't fight it.

6. MARKETING TACTIC-FOCUSED CLIENTS

These people are wired to understand where to place their bets in terms of the different types of marketing investments. Questions are more focused around when a particular marketing investment is increased or decreased, and their related impact.

Analytic requests from marketing tactic–focused clients might be in the form of setting up test and control groups where you can assess the value of a particular tactic. Seeing visual proof of whether a promotional effort is working is very important for this type of client. They want to see whether investments look like they are paying off. Based on the visual evidence of how tactics are performing, they can adjust their investments accordingly.

In a recent example, a test and control cell was designed with similar profiles and similar week-to-week performance prior to tactic deployment. If the tactic was successful there would be a trend break in the post-period (i.e., start of tactic) from the test versus control. Based on this cumulative gap week-to-week or month-to-month, incremental sales versus incremental cost can be calculated and updated as new data becomes available.

Marketing tactic-focused clients are similar to financially-focused clients, however marketing tactic-focused clients want to dig deeper into the detail on the tactic performance and even try to diagnose why that tactic works or doesn't work.

Challenges are similar for both client types, as you want to be knowledgeable about the cost related metrics. An additional wrinkle is that when you're dealing with a marketing tactic-focused individual, they are usually *in marketing*. As a result, when analyzing a particular tactic that this individual believes in, it can become quite challenging when the analysis points to the fact their tactic doesn't appear to work. In their mind your analysis must be in error, as they know the tactic "has to have worked." As an analyst, you need to understand the different marketing levers and associated metrics that are used in your business in order to be effective when having conversations with marketing tactic–focused clients.

7. SALES FORCE-FOCUSED CLIENTS

Similar to marketing-focused clients, these clients have a variety of metrics they like to follow around sales force engagement. These might entail the time salespeople are spending making sales calls. Where are they spending their time? Who are they targeting? How often?

A client who is more sales force–focused may want to see if the targets they've been given for a particular effort are getting the proper attention. This is sometimes summarized in a reach and frequency report. Reach—in the sales force context—is defined as the percent of targets that have been contacted over a certain period of time. Frequency is defined as the number of times a particular target was contacted over that same period of time. For example, a sales representative may have 100 targets. Segment A might be considered the most valuable of these targets, Segment B the next best, down to Segment D.

A particular sales rep may have 15 Segment As, 25 Segment Bs, 35 Segment Cs, and 25 Segment Ds.

A reach and frequency table would show the number of targets, the percent reached, and the average number of times each target was called on. Let's say for the most recent quarter you observed the following:

Segment	Targets	Reach	Frequency
A	15	93%	4
B	25	92%	3
C	35	94%	3
D	25	88%	2

Sales force–focused clients may have expectations of reach and or frequency. They might expect that all "A" targets are reached and "B" targets reach should be running at least 95 percent, with a frequency of at least four calls per target in a quarter. In short, these client types might like to look for sales areas where those expectations are not being met, and the reasons why.

Knowing the metrics these clients like to follow and understanding their patterns is essential to making the client/analyst connection. Get familiar with this jargon, as well as understanding the details of each of the metrics the client tends to reference.

The final two types of clients are extremely challenging, as they may fall into one of the aforementioned categories, but their approach and/or mindset can be tough, bordering on frustrating, for the analyst. Overcoming this frustration while providing good analytic support requires special concentration and patience.

8. "THE SIEVE"

The Sieve is a client who comes back from a meeting where they've jotted down the questions they were asked, and then pass these questions off to you, practically verbatim and with almost no context or explanation. Oh, and they need the answers quickly. When you press for more color around the questions, you pretty much get, "I don't know, just fill the request." My advice here is to try to not get caught up in how this person is delivering the request—just do your best to help them out. Chances are they may not be super comfortable with their role in the whole process either. They could be working for a difficult boss who isn't really explaining much, or the client themselves is really not happy in their own job and is just "checking the boxes." As you start to put things together and they see what you've come up with, you may find that your client becomes a little more engaged in giving some direction. However, if the habit continues and you're overwhelmed with requests, you may have to push back a bit and/or let your boss know you could use some cover.

9. BUILD MY SLIDES

There are going to be clients who feel that you're there to put together all their slides and fill in the numbers in templates for them. While I do believe analysts need to deliver analytic slides (I talk about this in Chapter 11), this is a tough one when it gets out of hand. My take here is that I generally will try to help out when I can, especially if I understand the context. I've done plenty of manual template filling within reason, and I try to send slides summarizing findings. If I know these types of requests are going to come often, I try to think of ways to automate them to make the process less painful. Each individual analyst has to make a call as to what they consider reasonable and unreasonable analytic requests. While unpleasant, if you can just bite the bullet once in a while, you may be able to work it out down the road. However, if you feel it's out of hand, having a conversation with that individual first is recommended. If that doesn't work, ask your boss what they think.

10. DEATH BY SCENARIO MARIO

This is a client type that feels that unless they have gone down every possible path they can think of, they won't be able to make a decision. They create a dynamic commonly referred to as "analysis paralysis."[8] The thinking is simple: I just can't decide until I know what happens when this happens. And if that happens, what happens then, and so on. I found that this client type generally has a fear that they will make a decision based on the data, miss something, and be vilified for it. This type of client is very challenging, as they have no problem asking for almost every permutation of an analysis. From the analyst's standpoint it seems like a very wide net.

One approach for the analyst is to pull back a bit and ask the client if they can be more specific about the objective and what is their biggest concern. Sometimes if you understand that a little better, you might be able to capture the different scenarios in one analysis. For example, a client might want a forecast, but realizes things could go better or worse than expected. Instead of treating this as three separate exercises (i.e., expected, better than expected, worse than expected), is there a way to create some parameter (or parameters) that when you move them up or down, they can see the movement of the assumptions in real time (maybe in an Excel spreadsheet)? This visual data interaction will give them an understanding of how the output changes when the parameters change. It might also help them get closer to what they're comfortable with. It is their way of making decisions. It may take a little more work and ingenuity on your end, but once you've done it the first time, you can be sure you'll probably reuse that approach again. In other cases, the client may be just buying time and the analyst can get burned out. It's important to set expectations of what you will and won't do. As always, make a study of this and see if there is some pattern in the request you could automate or capture. Challenge yourself after the exercise ends and ask if there is a way in the future to minimize the effort involved. This type of encounter will likely occur again.

---

[8] H. Igor Ansoff, *Corporate Strategy: an Analytic Approach to Business Policy for Growth and Expansion*, (New York: McGraw-Hill, 1965).

The bottom line is that, as an analyst, you need to go beyond just thinking about taking and fulfilling requests. To be truly effective, you need to also make a study of your clients and understand how they think and how they're wired. In short, if you can get into their shoes while providing good analytic support, you will most likely find that you'll feel less like a request taker and more like a collaborator.

CHAPTER 6

THE USUAL SUSPECTS

Let's come back to the team we talked about in Chapter 1. The team leader was frustrated to see the business showing flat performance. He wanted to know why it was like that and what to do about it, but the data the team presented didn't get at that information. He asked the team to frame the next meeting around those two specific areas.

After the meeting, the marketing head asks a marketing team member and analyst to stay behind to debrief. As they sit down, the marketing lead laments the meeting.

"We keep putting the same slides up and we're telling the same story each week, which is essentially no story: this is up, this is down. In the North growth is 3 percent, but in the South it's only 1 percent. Our top customers drive 40 percent of our business and have a 35 percent market share over the last year." Pausing for a moment, the marketing lead's frustration comes to the surface when she says, "If we can't really figure out what's going on and what to do about it, what's the point of having all these databases and fancy systems?"

After a few seconds, the analyst, also frustrated, says, "Isn't the point of the review to go through how each of the different metrics are behaving?"

"Yes," the marketing lead responds, "but that is only one part of what needs to be done. We also need to focus the review on the key issues or we shouldn't be putting those in the main presentation slides. There's got to be more of a story." She stands up to leave, but not before reiterating, "Let's focus on where we really think the problem lies and what action we're proposing, based on the results of the analysis."

Behind this conversation and the frustration there is an important impasse. Both the marketer and the analyst are thinking about two different things: the analyst is thinking about all the work they've already done, and the marketer is thinking about the work that hasn't been done yet.

The marketer is thinking, "I wish they would understand the position I'm in. I'd like for the analyst to help me get to the solution by jumping into my shoes for a minute. They deliver the data and then wish me well. I realize it takes time and effort to pull this together, but I'm not sure what I'm supposed to do with all these different reports I'm sent. As a result, it's hard for me to build the story."

The analyst is thinking, "Pulling all this data together and then summarizing is no easy task. I'm not sure marketing gets that. I don't always have the answers they're looking for and feel like they should be helping me help them with the story. They ask for a particular analysis and when I provide the results, and it doesn't satisfy, the results get dismissed. This is very irritating after I've spent time pulling this together."

The fact is they both have legitimate beefs. So, what are some ways to help bridge the divide and focus on the business issue at hand?

Each person must understand where the other might be struggling and make a conscious effort to help. On the marketing side, it is always helpful to frame how you might want to tell (or pace) the story, even though you don't have all the components of that story yet. For example, put together slides where the main problem is discussed, maybe even how long that problem has been "on the radar." Create a slide and/or template that has been effectively used in the past. Take a look at other presentations that have been previously done internally. Match the business problem with the metrics and segments that might have something to do with that problem. In other words, for the particular problem, what are the metrics that come to mind as the first ones to start looking at? In the current example there is a geographical sales component. What are the sales geographies? Is there anything to see by regions, territories, sales divisions, or sales areas? Does anything stand out by performance? What different customer types are typically looked at? Are there different promotional efforts in some of these sales areas or customer segments? What are the first metrics and/or segments that are most top of mind when you think about it for a moment?

These "whats" are what I like to call the "Usual Suspects." Thinking clearly about this list, even putting a placeholder in a deck, so that you've called it out directly.

By identifying these Usual Suspects combined with an upfront slide framework, you are narrowing the focus and serving up the problem in more of a step-by-step fashion.

On the analyst side, using this more focused framework will help the marketing folks tell more of a story once they get something that looks like a qualified lead from one of the Usual Suspects. The Usual Suspects, combined with the telling of a story, is just another way of saying the "whats," "whys," and "hows" or hitting the Analytic Trifecta. This pursuit of the story is as much the analyst's job as it is marketing's, and as an analyst, you need to keep this in mind. You don't want to get too stuck in request fulfillment mode.

Sometimes you may even posit a theory on a Not-So Usual Suspect. Not-So Usual Suspects may be something either very endemic to the specific business you're working with, or an area that is important, but doesn't always come to mind at first. Not-So Usual Suspects could also transcend traditional metrics and be something akin to an "out-of-the-box" idea or approach. Based on how certain client types think about the business, one person's Not-So Usual Suspect is another's Usual Suspect. This is why, as an analyst, soliciting ideas from different client types, that we mentioned in the previous chapter, makes you much more well-rounded in terms of analyzing the key business problems. I will give an example of the Usual and Not-So Usual Suspects later in the chapter.

"Both the marketer and the analyst are thinking about two different things: the analyst is thinking about all the work they've already done, and the marketer is thinking about the work that hasn't been done yet."

Another aspect of this relationship between client and analyst is to always keep the conversation going. Brainstorm different hypotheses within the Usual Suspects (or Not-So Usual Suspects) construct, but the client needs to be mindful of the fact that not every avenue can be pursued by the analyst, and you don't want to overwhelm them. Try keeping things focused.

Both parties should think through, "If I find this, then what would the next step be?" If that next step might not lead anywhere compelling, don't pursue it. That dead-end path might not be obvious until you talk it through, so it's worth having the conversation.

It's easy for a client to cast a wide net and say, "Let's look at everything," or, "What are the key performance indicators (KPIs) telling us?" To the analyst this sounds like, "Go figure it out." It also may be demotivating for the analyst, as they are usually looking for more concrete direction. If you're both actively invested and thinking through the problem at hand, the interaction will be much more fruitful. It also doesn't hurt to recognize good effort on both sides. For example, as a client, it is always a good idea to take time to recognize the analyst's effort and show appreciation if they are clearly trying to pull all this information together and summarize what they've found. There will be many findings that won't lead anywhere, however the analyst still had to spend energy and time on what ultimately arrived at a dead-end.

On the analyst side, recognize when the client is making an effort to focus the work. In addition, if they come up with a good way of summarizing findings or what you think is a good idea, show appreciation as well, maybe by saying something like, "That's a good way to show that. I like that approach. That helps me focus."

Let's go back to the "sales are flat" meeting where the franchise head wanted some answers, and see how we can start looking at the Usual Suspects and possibly Not-So Usual Suspects. From some of the data that was already presented at that initial meeting, there were some clues. The top customers were moving in the positive direction for our competitor. There were declines in the Southwest portion of the West region.

Sometimes when the focus of your analysis is through the lens of your own product you might miss something important about your competitor. Given that the new competitor is doing well, it might make more sense to think of the Usual Suspects from the competitor's lens.

Do we have information on what percent of business my competitor gets by state? Who are their top customers? Can we look at their business by our sales regions? From our own product's point of view, do we know what the sales calls in the Southwest were over the time period before this product launched and currently?

When we pull our sales call information by state, we see that two weeks prior to our competitor's launch, our sales calls declined dramatically and only returned to much lower levels recently. This is the "what."

Now for the "why." Why did sales calls decline so dramatically? We did hear during the meeting that there was "some turnover in that area." Can this be confirmed? Making a call over to the sales team we discover that Stephanie, a salesperson who had been in that area for three years left and her replacement started a week ago. We asked if they knew where Stephanie might have gone. They think she went to work for the competitor. When we pull state-by-state information on our competitor, we get the following chart:

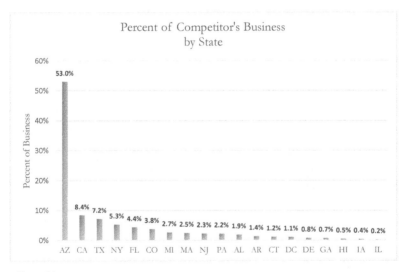

Figure 6.1

It's surprising that the competitor is so concentrated in Arizona (53 percent of their business). Given the timing of Stephanie's departure, she alone wouldn't completely explain the concentration of business.

As the analyst and marketer comb through this deeper dive level information, they sense a story developing. The analyst and the marketer together are now looking for Not-So Usual suspects. They do an online search on the competitor product name and Arizona. What they find is startling. They see the following announcement dated four months prior to the competitor's product launch:

Pierre Poacherre has joined [the competitor]. He was previously at NEI (our company) for seven years. He is originally from Arizona and has moved back to the area.

$$\bullet \; \bullet \; \bullet$$

As they both stare at each other, they realize that Pierre is behind the strong launch and has strong customer relationships in Arizona. He left our company about a year ago and no one knew where he went. It appears he convinced Stephanie to cover those local customers. Pierre was most likely working his hometown area customers a few months before this competitive product was launched. He also knows the strengths and weaknesses of our product very well.

With this information, they realize that they now have a big part of the story.

The "what:" Business is flat and some portion of that seems to be fueled from the Southwest. Arizona in particular.

The "why:" Lost an experienced salesperson in Arizona who joined our competitor. The competitor's new head of marketing is also a former employee.

The "how:" First we need to bring this information to the team lead and suggest we connect with customers who went to the competitor.

As you can see from this "what," "why," and "how" exercise, the Usual Suspects (though a more focused subset) got things started, which led to a journey where the "why" was bouncing the analytic information off of people in the know (sales). This in turn substantiated some of the theories. Ultimately working together and thinking more about the "why" led to a Not-So Usual online search result that delivered a startling finding and helped round out the story.

In short, start with the Usual Suspects and think through the questions. As you work your way through the answers, your analysis should lead you in the right direction to begin building the story.

Not-So Usual Suspects are always worth considering, as well. Focusing deeper on which of the suspects might be leaving clues and having an interactive discussion with those who are more knowledgeable about that area of the business is also critical to help unravel the mystery.

As with any detective work, there is no promise that all clues will always lead to a definitive and helpful insight. Approaching the problem working the Usual Suspects will surely lead you on a journey that will most likely fill in some of the pieces of the puzzle.

CHAPTER 7

STAY IN YOUR LANE,
GET OUT OF THE CAVE

Your approach to any analytic challenge says a lot about the type of analyst you are. While you may find the area of analytics interesting or even fascinating, your attitude and how you communicate the results of what you've found make a bigger impression on those you support than you might realize. One of the more popular dichotomies I've seen is that of the proactive versus the reactive analyst.

At its core, the reactive analyst is someone who is waiting for requests to get their day started; their level of activity is generally ruled by their client's level of request activity.

The proactive analyst is not only waiting for requests, but is also constantly thinking about the business and how they can help answer what they consider the critical business questions.

Typically, the proactive analyst is more desirable. However, there are many situations that are better suited for the reactive analyst. In fact, a successful analyst should have an idea what's called for depending on the situation. There are also some other analytic behaviors that analysts may find themselves emulating, and each one has its pros and cons.

In addition to the reactive and proactive analytic types, I am adding two more analytic behaviors: the directive analyst and the reclusive analyst.

THE FOUR
ANALYTIC BEHAVIORS

1. The reactive analyst generally perceives their role as one of request fulfillment. In many circumstances, reactive analysts see the requests they receive as a technical challenge that they can apply their database knowledge and software or coding skills to, aka the type of work they were built to do. Taking a request and being able to technically navigate that request using the analytic software across multiple databases and output results is an impressive skill. In fact, many reactive analysts feel that the main measurement of their success is the accurate and timely turnaround of requests. They enjoy the positive feedback they get from turning things around quickly, and their clients appreciate the role they play. These individuals generally work well under pressure, and in many cases, they can be very productive. However, it is this focus on productivity that sometimes limits them when it comes to really thinking through what the results are saying.

As we discussed in the "whats," "whys," and "hows" of analytics in Chapter 1, the "what" is simply asking the question, "What does the data show?" "Show me the numbers. Put it in a report or graph." This requires the ability to pull the required data and summarize it. "What" questions are pretty direct in the sense that the visual on the deliverable is usually clear, regardless of the difficulty of pulling and summarizing that data.

The "why" question is immediate, and occurs once someone looks at those numbers and notices some pattern. "Why is this happening?" This is more of an open-ended question, and there is not a clear path on where to go next.

The reactive analyst struggles with the "why" question for a number of reasons. First and foremost, they are in their comfort zone in the "what" (clear deliverable) lane, and don't see the "why" as part of their job. Additionally, they might be very inexperienced on the business side and/ or don't generally ask others for feedback on the "why." What I've found is that people who become really good at reacting to requests, at some point are looking for something more than just request fulfillment and a pat on the back. They know the data probably better than most and want something a little more challenging. The problem is that they haven't had much practice thinking and working through the "whys." In addition, while clients really appreciate the responsiveness, they privately wish these analysts were thinking more about the implications of their results and even taking the next step on their own. Some clients feel they have to map everything out in great detail in order to get the results they need. In short, the responsiveness of the reactive analyst is desired and appreciated, but they need to swim in the "why" lane if and when possible. It's okay to ask for help, and the water may be deeper, but it will help them develop into a stronger analyst.

2. The proactive analyst, in addition to working on direct requests, is thinking about what those results are telling them. They may also be doing analyses based on either their own theories or theories based on something they may have heard from their client, colleague, or at a meeting, without being prompted to do so.

With respect to the "what," "why," and "how" framework, the reactive analyst is for the most part working and thinking exclusively in the "what" lane, while the proactive analyst is working and thinking across all three.

The proactive analyst is that next step from just being reactive. This individual is not only considering the request, but how it fits into what they understand as part of the overall critical business questions. They are channeling the analytical investigative spirit. Requests are just a means to an end for them to figure out the "why" as part of the bigger picture, using the data to help shape the answer.

So, what could possibly be the downside of being a proactive analyst? Sometimes, taking the results of the data analysis to the next step may not be what your client is really looking for. They may see you as moving the work to somewhere they didn't intend or feel that you might be stepping in their area of expertise. I recall a meeting a while back where a particular head of marketing was frustrated with someone trying to drive their strategy based on the analysis they did in their specialized, non-marketing role. As we were walking down the hall, I remember him saying that "So-and-so should stay in their lane!" I found the metaphor funny, but also realized that sometimes, without knowing it, the proactive analyst can veer into someone else's lane. Worse yet, proactive analysts can get so caught up in all the possibilities, that they not only veer out of their swim lane, but exit the pool, and end up in a remote forest.

As a proactive analyst you have to know your boundaries ("Stay in your lane!") and make sure you're riding with, and supporting your client, rather than driving them. Always probe and ask what they think first. It doesn't mean that you should stop thinking proactively, but you also have to realize what is required at that moment.

3. The directive analyst is someone who sees an analytic request as something that needs to be managed carefully up-front, usually with a timeline and deliverable. It's also possible that based on what they already know about the data, they may even recommend against and/or redirect the effort; they don't want to necessarily react or proact *just yet*. They want to fully understand the objective of the request and be able to direct those expectations up-front. These analysts want to be certain about what they can deliver, and are concerned about the commitment of resources and the costs of analytic efforts. Instead of the "what," "why," and "how," they are thinking about the "who" and "when." Specifically, who is going to do the work, and when are the results expected?

Directive analysts are also sensitive to ensuring the time dedicated to an analytic effort is well spent. They want to probe a little more up-front and understand what actions will be taken based on specific outcomes. They don't want to go down too many rabbit holes with nothing to show for it, so they're more *proactive* in managing the request. If the intent is strictly to get things really focused up-front, that is a positive, but the directive analyst has to be careful not to become too rigid.

They can be perceived as an analytic stop sign, turning every request into a project. If done adeptly, the directive analyst can help the client think more carefully about what they're ultimately looking for, especially clients who are little less experienced in their area, or are looking for some ideas about which analytic approach to take. However, this more experienced analyst can sometimes be too direct and close out other paths for analysis. As is their namesake, directive analysts are usually pretty direct about the results as well. They sometimes convey that what they've put together is the only way to look at the problem, and there's really nothing more to investigate.

If they are more open, while trying to direct analyses to a place both the analyst and client are comfortable, the search for results may proceed more efficiently.

4. The reclusive analyst is one who, when working on a request, likes to put all their effort into the analysis without any distractions. Once they know what the ask is, they typically go into what I call the "analytical cave" to get their work done. The analytic work requires a good deal of concentration for them, and they want, and may even enjoy, working in solitude.

This analyst type likes analytic questions they can sink their teeth into. However, they want a good deal of time to work on these big questions. Additionally, they don't want to be bothered and like to hole up in a quiet space with their computer. This is the classic stereotype of the introverted analyst. They may be more advanced in their analytic knowledge and are happy to have a discussion about the big problem at hand. Their focus can sometimes generate very well thought out and valuable insights. However, when they are working on a request, they prefer to "go into a cave" and not come out until they're done with the work. The problem with this approach is that things can, and usually do change along the way with either a subtle or material alteration in the request. When this happens, the client doesn't always want to take the time for a cave visit to communicate the latest changes. They also don't want to deal with the expected analyst blowback, especially when the analyst is so intensely focused on the original request. The client may let the original analysis play out and see if there are any insights they can use once the results are presented. If they do communicate the change in direction, the reclusive analyst's reaction is usually one of, "I have to start all over again?" They're often frustrated that the client changed their mind, and see this as the client not knowing what they want, or that the client doesn't really know what their *boss* wants. The reality is that the business moves quickly, and what was critical last week has been replaced by something more critical this week. In fact, last week's critical may no longer be relevant.

The bottom line here is don't be too much of an analytic cave dweller. Yes, you need to focus and have uninterrupted time to do good analytic work, but you also must keep in contact (quick informal "touch point" meetings), so if things change, you're in the know.

The four analytic behaviors (proactive, reactive, directive, and reclusive) are not a mutually exclusive and exhaustive list. At different points in time an analyst can move between them. Each one has its pros and cons, and a strong analyst learns which elements of each to use and when, as they are keenly aware of how their clients tend to react to each. This skill will make you the best analyst type of them all: The Adaptive Analyst.

ANALYTIC BEHAVIOR	PROS	CONS
REACTIVE	Gets things done. Works well under pressure. Turns around requests quickly.	Doesn't really pursue answering the "why" question based on their analyses.
PROACTIVE	Same as reactive, but thinks through not only the request itself but what the client/business is ultimately looking for. Curious to help answer the "why" questions as they come up. Connects with other experts in other groups for input.	Can potentially push the analysis to another place away from client's focus. Unwanted encroachment into client's area of expertise.
DIRECTIVE	Looks to make efficient use of analytic resource/cost. Can help direct better approach to analyses based on their experience.	Can sometimes be perceived as an analytic stop sign. Manages requests too rigidly.
RECLUSIVE	Very focused/deep thinking on the big requests, which may generate valuable insights. Does not get distracted from request objective.	Doesn't adapt well to changes in the requests. Disconnected from the day-to-day.

CHAPTER 8

CAN SOMEONE INTERPRET THIS FOR ME...PLEASE?

There is no doubt that the amount of data available and the ability to extract information from these data sources more quickly, continue to grow. There are many more software packages in the market that not only crunch data well but offer quick graphics and nice visuals, too. Additionally, there seems to be no shortage of new analytic jargon—from big data, use cases, data lakes, machine learning, data science, the list goes on.... You can also find all sorts of conferences on analytics that seem to be happening weekly. There are even billboards on the interstates that advertise courses in analytics!

However, with all of this training about working with data using the latest technology and analytic techniques, there continues to be one important subtle piece missing. There is still a quiet frustration on the client side with getting key insights they can really use. There's no doubt these clients get a lot of data, but it is not always synthesized into the form that they need to digest it.

Data summaries arrive as some set of reports, spreadsheets, and/or dashboards, and clients struggle with trying to understand what the key findings are. No, the clients are not dumb or lazy (which I've heard analysts say). They want to get to the key findings, and don't want to have to wade through an analytic forest to get there. They'd like that analyst to help focus them or what they think stands out.

When a variety of spreadsheets, reports, and dashboards are sent out, the client's perception is that the analyst is saying to them, "Here are all the tasty ingredients. Pick what you'd like and go cook something up." In many places, this type of interaction is common and the client tends to adjust to this style. In fact, many clients have had to (by necessity) become more versant in going through a lot of data summaries to figure out what might be occurring that's important. Privately they indicate their frustration with this analytic process, and they don't always know how to get the message across without upsetting the analyst. When a deadline looms, the frustration can surface directly on both analyst and client sides.

Analysts, in addition to trying to address the questions at hand, are thinking about ways to improve their processing, analysis, and even visualization of the data. Automating a process for sending out large amounts of data to a large number of end users can save time. End users however often find that one-size-fits-all reports may give them some good information but doesn't address their specific questions. Additionally, those questions will invariably create other questions once they're answered. As a result, it is common that business questions needing an answer can't directly be answered by all the different reports, dashboards, and spreadsheets provided.

Analytic types can spend too much time with other analytic types. I've seen analytic software presentations where you hear, "Wow, that's a really cool way to do that or show that." The client may agree, but when they get back to their desk, that coolness doesn't actually help them answer the questions their boss needs answers to.

DASHBOARDS, SCORECARDS, SCOREBOARDS

One of the more popular ways to summarize a variety of different information in one place is typically distilled into an information dashboard, scorecard, or scoreboard. The information dashboard is probably the most popular term, but you will sometimes hear the terms scorecard or scoreboard. All three are different consolidated visualizations of key statistics. The basic idea is to display some basic statistics or key performance indicators on one page, so that it's easy to see everything at a glance. Dashboards combine different graphic representations of the data. You will typically see various chart types (e.g., bar charts, pie charts, line charts, doughnut charts, speedometer charts, area charts, etc.), tables, numbers in larger font that stand out, maybe even a map. Usually, these dashboards are colorful and have some nice brand or company logo in the corner to give it that customized newsletter look. Ideally, they are designed in such a way that each of the dashboard panels can be automatically updated when new data become available.

There is a good deal of effort to design these dashboards to get as much information onto a page as possible. Adding drop-down menus and radio buttons, for example, allows the casual user to interact with different views of the data by selecting different combinations of each variable.

All of this sounds great. It may even look very pleasing, when you're exposed to some of the initial dashboards. However, once the (non-scripted) questions come in, the dashboard probably won't help much. This is not to say that the dashboard doesn't provide value, and may help with some deeper-level questions, but more often than not, the dashboard is very limited.

One of the patterns that I've noticed with many dashboards is that much of the real estate on the page is taken up with graphics that convey just one number. Common examples are doughnut charts or speedometer charts.

Below is nice sized doughnut (chart) declaring 45 percent market share for our product.

NEI Product Market Share is now 45%

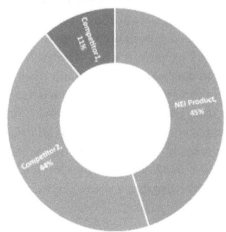

A very simplified speedometer chart below shows sales volume hit 65K for the fourth quarter.

Sales Volume was 65K for Q4

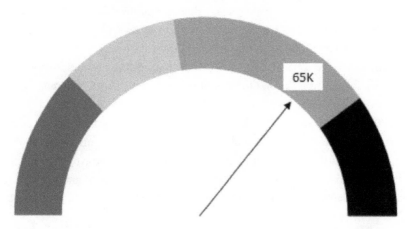

These two panels may be pleasing to look at, but they take up a lot of real estate on the dashboard. I've seen folks spend a good deal of time building much more sophisticated graphics of this type so that when new data comes in, the graphics update nicely. Bottom line: it's helpful to know the numbers. Clients might not need the pretty colors or shapes, especially after seeing this dashboard more than a few times a month.

Stephen Few's book *Information Dashboard Design: The Effective Visual Communication of Data* talks about the "13 mistakes of common dashboard design" and discusses how to make dashboards more effective.[9]

Another example I see often is when different line charts are fit and compressed onto the dashboard page, and as a result every trend looks mostly flat for one or two reasons. The first reason is that the chart becomes so small you can't really read it. The second reason is that there might be one line that so dominates the others, you can't tell what's going on with the other lines. As a result, they're either buried or they look flat. Even if there's an ability to expand the size of the charts, the quick at a glance visual leads the user to believe there's nothing to see here.

---

[9] Stephen Few, *Information Dashboard Design: The Effective Visual Communication of Data* (Newton: O'Reilly, 2006).

Here is the chart as it appears on the dashboard:

Quarterly Sales Volume

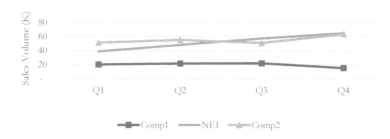

With the battle for dashboard real estate, it looks like the NEI product and Competitor 2 are pretty close to each other, and there looks like a mild decline in Competitor 1. When I don't have to force the chart into a small area, I can see a little more going on at a glance.

Quarterly Sales Volume

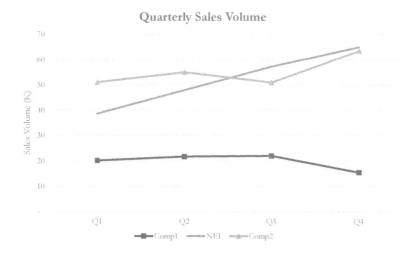

Competitor 1 is declining a little more dramatically, and NEI's trajectory looks the strongest.

Here's the second example where a dominant product dwarfs the others:

Product 2 is doing better than Product 3. Gaps look to be widening a little.

Now when the chart is not compressed, and the axes are adjusted to focus on Products 2 and 3, you see a much more dramatic picture. Product 2 has now more than *triple* Product 3's market share.

In Darrell Huff's book *How to Lie with Statistics*, the author talks about the "Gee Whiz Graph," whereby expanding the y-axis, you could make things look really dramatic, or by compressing the y-axis make things look very uneventful.[10] The important thing to focus on is the y-axis itself, and to judge whether trends are truly meaningful.

Dashboards, scorecards, or scoreboards can be very enticing to design, set up code, and have a quick automated update process. I'm a big believer in the fact that it's important to keep score and summarize the key metrics.

---

[10] Darrell Huff, *How to Lie with Statistics* (New York: W. W. Norton, 1954), 62.

Anyone watching a sporting event usually wants to know the score as well as looking at some other statistics during, and maybe even before and after the event. However, the really good sports analyst will not just quote those numbers but will give you insight into why it is happening and how can it be improved or changed. They will also simultaneously explain it in such a way that you can understand it and get a deeper appreciation for what's happening, without too much inside or technical jargon.

When clients are more analytically oriented, such as the ones mentioned in Chapter 5 (detailed data–focused or summary data–focused), they might like the dashboards in addition to getting summary data spreadsheets. They might also take charge of the analytic insights. As a result, the analyst is playing more of the tool developer or designer role. From the analyst's standpoint, as mentioned previously, you want to make sure you're not painted solely into the tool designer/updater role. This can be avoided by making sure that, as an analyst, you analyze and think about the data on your own so you're part of the analytic insight finding.

"As an effective business analyst, you are the analytic translator."

One other dynamic about any dashboards, scorecards, scoreboards, or reports in general is being aware and cluing in end-users of data "watch-outs." For the data in general or specific attributes here are some examples of things to watch out for:

- Is the information current? As of what date?
- Are specific attributes less current than others? When are they updated?

- Are the most recent data points reliable or do they tend to change when there is an update?
- Are certain segment sample sizes so small that I should be careful interpreting trends or patterns?

As I mentioned earlier, databases don't usually come with good data dictionaries or even a basic operating manual, so too is the case with dashboards. Casual users often don't know certain things that the analyst might know, and as a result take the trends at face value. I've seen this happen with "transactional" or "reported cases" data. The last one or two data points are not complete. This occurs as the reporting sources/systems for whatever reason typically are run anywhere from one to two data periods behind (or lagged), sometimes more, before the results for that period are complete. The end-user of this data (who is not aware of this data lag), immediately notices a visual pattern and may ring the alarm bells that something bad is happening. If you know the data is incomplete, why put it out there? If there is a systematic (predictable) understatement of recent data points, better to either put the observation out with its predicted value (with a footnote), so at least you can give some guidance on the most recent data, or only present data up to the last fully baked data point.

In short, dashboards may give clients a quick overview of some of the "what" part of the data. They serve the purpose of showing information at a glance.

What these dashboards or scorecards sometimes become is a template for either analytics support groups or IT to try to squeeze even more types of automated information into a finite space. The thinking is that if the client has asked for it at one time, it might be worth automating into the dashboard, and as an analyst, you're capturing the latest thinking.

Trying to track every type of question in hopes of anticipating all future questions usually doesn't work out that well in practice. (Having said that, it doesn't stop teams from trying.) Unfortunately, there is always some unexpected nuance in the way questions arrive and the answers don't directly reside on the dashboard.

The other danger of spending too much time "feeding the dashboard" is that the client gets frustrated that they're put in a position where they're supposed to figure out what all the dashboard dials are *really* telling them and why. This is more pronounced when the dashboards themselves get even busier. They might appreciate the effort to get everything on one page, but in order to make decisions they need more of the interpretation.

What does all this information mean? It's not enough to say, "This metric looks healthy, this one doesn't." Why? Can you interpret what I'm looking at? Is everything I need to know about, in the dashboard?

Think of a car's dashboard. It has a lot of information, and in severe cases will pop up important warnings (sometimes referred to as "idiot lights"). However, driving the car using only the dashboard is clearly dangerous, and the driver also knows that they have to navigate and adjust to what they are seeing through the windows and mirrors in real time. As their experience grows, they get a sense of which information to focus on and which changes in information are of concern.

As an effective business analyst, you are the **analytic translator**. You can see the dashboard, but you also have insight into information that can't be quickly stuck into the dashboard template. If you're also in touch with the business, you are getting a fuller picture of what's happening and are in a position to interpret what you're seeing from this broader view.

This doesn't imply that you have all the answers, but the fact that you're making an attempt to interpret the whats and whys from all this information is not only what your client is looking for, but the business as well.

CHAPTER 9

RANSOM NOTE SPREADSHEETS

There is no doubt that most, if not all, of the analytic results you produce will be summarized and delivered to your client via e-mail. When you're sending these results back to your client, they're reading and digesting what you've found as if you're talking with them directly. How you summarize your analytic findings is just as important as what you've found. It also conveys your general style of communication around analytic deliverables.

We all have different styles of writing e-mail, and I'm not looking to posit a best approach, however there are a few e-mail styles that have that "data dump," "order fulfillment," or "I'm really busy with other important stuff" feel about it.

I find that even though in some cases it's okay to just send a quick data sheet over-the-fence, especially if you're really crunched for time and the recipient at that other end just needs numbers to plug in somewhere ("cut-and-paste job"), it's not a good habit to get into.

I've found the best way to send over analytic results is to first write up the key highlights summarized in body of the e-mail. If you can put key takeaways in bullet form, that's usually easy to read. The e-mail shouldn't be too wordy; just get to the point. If you're attaching data in a spreadsheet, give a quick explanation of what it contains. Have the title of the sheet convey that, as well.

Always keep in mind that if you include a nice easy-to-follow and succinct written summary of your analysis in the body of your e-mail, and accompany that analysis with helpful attachments, you are demonstrating to others your overall style in how you deliver analytic results.

If that isn't persuasive, you might want to consider that well written analytic results e-mails will most likely get forwarded and may make their way to higher level individuals within the organization, who will take notice of your name, and the results *you* found. If they don't know you, your analytic results e-mail will be your introduction.

I would also consider the fact that if you've spent a good deal of time on the analysis, it's worth the effort to also have a clear summary of what you found in the body of the e-mail. If you're attaching a spreadsheet and/or PowerPoint slides, you want them to be clear as well. Remember, you're talking directly to the recipient/client through these results deliverable e-mails.

In many analyses the common analytic deliverable after some analytic work is done, is to summarize the data into a spreadsheet and save the file as the default Excel name "Book1.xlsx" or "Book2.xlsx." It doesn't seem like a big deal, but why not give the file a name describing what the file is about? It won't take much extra time, especially given the work you've done. In the long run, naming files in a more descriptive way helps you and your client keep track of the data.

One example of an analytic deliverable that typically irritates clients arises when there is a direct request for some analysis, with a specific focus on a receiving a fair amount of data. When the e-mail is sent out the results are displayed in the body of the e-mail as a picture only and there is no workable data attachment. Usually when folks are asking for a set of numbers, they would like the ability to not have to retype them into their own spreadsheet. This gives rise to the inevitable return e-mail question, "Can you put the data in a spreadsheet so I can work with it?" The return e-mail attachment: "Book1.xlsx."

Another example is what I like to call the "ransom note" spreadsheet or e-mail. Back in the low-tech days, ransom notes were constructed by taking words or letters from newspapers or magazines, piecing them together into sentences, and sending these notes out so that the person sending the note's handwriting couldn't be traced. An example might look something like this:

Growth must surpass 2.5% by next Friday.

I have seen spreadsheets where the fonts in each column are different sizes, different styles, misaligned, or all three. Additionally, I have also seen e-mails where someone has cut and pasted numbers or text from different spreadsheets that had different font styles and sizes, and the resulting e-mail has that ransom note look to it. Sending information like this as the deliverable of your work inadvertently says something about your style.

It's important to remember that many people will look at your reports on smartphones and tablets. They might rarely open their laptops. When they receive an e-mail that has a PowerPoint attachment, for example, they are immediately frustrated that they can't really see the slides that well, or the graphics are not scaled or formatted correctly. I remember one executive who had one of the older iPhones and was always squinting to read all their e-mails. This person was always on the move and if they couldn't read something, they would ask their admin to print a hard copy of the attachment for them. If I had sent out an updated PowerPoint deck and they wanted to pull that information up, this person would look at me and yell, "I can't read what you sent on my phone!" They would then yell their admin's name to print a hard copy.

I realized that if I was sending PowerPoint slides, I should also attach a PDF version of those slides (PowerPoint has a "save as" option to do this). This approach for the most part, minimized some of that frustration. Once I started doing this, I realized this was also appreciated by those who were traveling—whether they were building slides or just viewing them—and it didn't cost me too much extra time to accommodate them.

This delivery of PowerPoint Slides in .pptx form versus PDF form raises another type of question that some analytic folks wrestle with. In a typical situation, a marketing person might ask the analyst to put some of their findings into a few PowerPoint slides. When the marketer receives those slides, they may like to "tweak" those slides. A tweak can go from changing some words in a title, moving items, shading out certain parts of a graph, or even deleting some stuff you deemed important like certain footnotes.

The person ultimately presenting the slides might even make edits without telling the analyst ahead of time. Sometimes the slides look different from what you've sent and an executive's question revolves around something that was edited or deleted. This event is definitely a "flop-sweat" moment as an analyst. You are not only confronted with a question that you are trying to answer, but you also are pretty ticked off that your slide was changed—sabotaged?—you didn't know about, and you want to yell out, "Why did you change my slide without telling me? I put all that info out there for a reason." I have been in this situation a number of times and always have my original reference slides as a backup if something big is changed.

After an experience like this the analyst may feel that from now on they will only send out PDFs so that the files are more difficult to edit. The marketer will most likely want PowerPoint slides, as they will want to edit or rearrange certain things. As the analyst, it never hurts to ask if you can get the final edits (if there are any) to the slides in advance of a key meeting, so you're not caught off guard. In this way you can find common ground beforehand. In most of my experiences when I have this interaction beforehand and I see the edits that they'd like to do, I definitely learn some techniques about how to make my slides better. It doesn't always happen, but most of the time I get a better understanding of how my client is thinking.

These are all important aspects of basic customer service. Of course, you want your analyses to be clear, helpful, insightful, and hopefully impactful, but execution on the delivery should also not be overlooked. Presentation matters. I myself have been on the receiving end and have been with others when they receive a picture e-mail, ransom note spreadsheet, a sloppy Book1.xls file, or PowerPoint deck they can't easily open on their smart devices, and have heard the "why couldn't they just send…" refrain. While there are apps that may overcome viewing problems, the typical user will not always want to take to time to learn how to do this. PDFs are safest because they display consistently across devices.

As an analyst, think a little more carefully on the analysis delivery and take those extra moments to check out the e-mail you're sending. Make sure it's clear and steers clear of some of the pet peeves mentioned here. You never know when one of your analysis e-mails will get forwarded and who may ultimately see it. Your name will be associated with it, so make sure to put your best (analytic e-mail) foot forward.

the RANSOM NOTE SPREADSHEET

CHAPTER 10

DETECTIVE SABOTAGE

After spending countless hours working on an analysis and standing up in front of an audience presenting those results, there's nothing more nerve-racking than hearing those words, "Are you sure those numbers are correct?" This statement alone is like having a monkey wrench thrown into your whole analysis.

Think about it. You've spent all this time trying to put together what you believe is a good summary of the analytic challenge at hand. You've also probably put a lot of thought into how to show those results visually in a series of slides, introducing the problem you're trying to solve, and hoping that the overall story flow and key takeaways generate a good discussion. Your analysis may even help inform an important decision. Then out of nowhere, you get derailed with a question that challenges that your numbers are even correct. If those numbers are some of the most critical numbers in your presentation, then the whole focus is now on whether you made some key errors, and whether your entire analysis is valid.

You don't want this to happen.

Are there steps you can take to avoid having this happen? What is the nature of the challenge? Did they see different numbers from someone or somewhere else? Are they doing some quick math and the numbers don't add up?

As an analyst you need to be critical of the numbers as well. By doing this before the presentation, you're less likely to have to fix mistakes later. Usually, the numbers disconnect challenge falls into two categories. They are either what I call, using the detective parlance, an "inside job" or an "outside job."

A numbers disconnect "inside job" is defined as what may appear to be the same exact group or segment showing different results, or something doesn't make sense from a math standpoint. In either case, the main reason that someone notices a potential disconnect for an "inside job" is that it is completely contained and created from numbers within your presentation.

As a simple example, I could have one slide that says that the West grew by 5 percent over the last year, but on a different slide it says the West grew by 10 percent. Can both be correct? If the time periods are different, then of course it's possible. Does "West" mean the same thing in both slides? If not, be specific about the different West segments and avoid the obvious and unnecessary confusion. If both West segments are the same thing, then there's obviously an error.

Another example is a math error or typo. For example, the rows or columns of the table that should add up, don't add up to the total, whether it's a volume total or percent total.

"Inside job" disconnects can be very simple to explain or be as complex as doing different analysis using separate data sources, where the same metric shows a different result. Whichever the case, you must make sure in advance that identical metrics are indeed identical, wherever they appear in your final analysis.

There are many people who, when they see a set of numbers or different numerical summaries, are wired to pressure test that those numbers make sense and don't disconnect in some way. They're not even listening to what you're saying. They are either taking out a calculator, or in their head they're checking all the math. It sometimes feels like they're excited if they can find an error in your presentation and point that out to the audience, so that someone can tell them, "Wow, good catch!" You can usually spot these individuals if you look carefully. They are the ones looking at your slide very intently, as if it's a bill they just received, and they want to make sure they haven't been overcharged. In short, "inside job" disconnects can be clearly pointed out from information contained inside your presentation deck. You must be the master of these potential disconnects, because if there are any, you created them.

I see "inside job" repair as akin to analytic proofreading. Check that columns and row totals add up and percentages that should sum to 100 percent add up to 100 percent. In addition, any sort of obvious errors with numbers such as having a slide that says the product is seeing 50 percent growth when you know that number is probably wrong, as growth rates for this product are generally in the mid-single to lower-double digits. You may realize that the 50 percent is a typo, and it should have been 5 percent. Take the extra effort on the "inside job" cleanup and repair to check your work.

A numbers disconnect "outside job" is defined as a disconnect between numbers that you're showing and numbers that exist outside of your presentation. The outside party is usually a person or group of people who are pointing out a discrepancy. Essentially, you're showing certain numbers to someone and it doesn't make sense to them. This could be based on what they already know about the business and/or they've seen these numbers presented by someone else previously, and they were different. It could be something as simple as they are questioning your data source and believe it is not accurate or trusted. In cases like this you want to resolve beforehand whether the data sources you're using are internal trusted sources.

Essentially, you have a challenge either from this individual directly or they're challenging you indirectly on what they remember seeing from someone/somewhere else. In some cases, they just may not like your conclusion, so they're looking for a critical numerical weakness in your analysis, or they just want to pressure-test your analysis, knowledge, and confidence in general.

This "outside job" disconnect can show up for many different reasons and may sometimes derail your entire analysis. No matter what, it's something you have to be ready for and have a way to deal with to get things back on track.

Before we get into how to handle the different situations that are most likely to occur, I'd like to confine the challenges to situations where the data is accessible within the company databases. This would exclude

situations where someone challenged your results based on something that someone said but couldn't replicate, or something they read in an article. Given this situation, let's talk about the different outcomes. There are only three, but there can be a lot going on underneath each one that goes way beyond right and wrong. The three outcomes are:

1. Someone's right and someone's wrong.
2. You're both correct. You're either not comparing similar things, or the approaches are different and yield different results.
3. You're both wrong. You both made a mistake or misunderstood the question and/or assumptions.

Conflicts usually come down to two basic questions:

1. What is the source for your information?
2. How are you making your calculations?

Table 10.1 below shows different types of data source conflicts

Some of these situations are more difficult to resolve as two different analytic approaches may seem acceptable, but give different results. If this is the source of the disconnect, you may have to consider results of both approaches, and make a call.

SOMEONE'S RIGHT AND SOMEONE'S WRONG

If you are presenting new numbers that happen to be in conflict with "outside" numbers, which may have been around for some time, you may be incorrect and the "outside" numbers are correct, or the reverse may be the case.

In the case where the "outside" numbers are correct and your numbers are not, there has at the least been some doubt cast on your analysis. If those numbers were critical to your conclusions, your analysis may be in serious doubt. Overall, it is not a pleasant experience, but one you should learn from and try to avoid in the future. Specifically, what was the source of the mistake? Was it data source related or calculation related?

Data Source Conflict for Certain Variables	Example
Internal trusted vs. external source	External: You're quoting an estimate of our monthly sales.
	Internal: We already know our actual monthly sales.
Trusted but not preferred internally	Company purchases two different data sources that have primary address information for prospects
	-Source A: primary address is in California,
	-Source B: primary address is in Nevada.
	-Source A is the preferred source internally.
Trusted but some variables are less accurate	Sales call activity each week is trusted, however the last two weeks are not accurate.
Trusted but not recent	You're quoting numbers from the January presentation. We have March numbers that are more current.

Calculation Conflict	Example
Different segment defintions	I calculated the percent of customers by state across the entire database. Database has all customer types. Did you use only active customers as of today?
Program coding differences or program errors	Have you double-checked your code and are the formulas you're using correct and/or consistent?
Different statistical techniques	Regression-based approach. Time-series approach.
Formula differences	I calculated based on a 2-year impact, you used a 3-year impact.

Table 10.1

Good advice for this situation is best captured by something John Wooden, the famous former UCLA college basketball coach, once said. He pointed out that, "Failing to prepare is preparing to fail."[11] Before you trot out any numbers, make sure you've checked them out, whether it's double-checking your programming, calculations, or bouncing those numbers off individuals who are more familiar with them. Don't assume the numbers must be right. Make sure they're right. It's always possible that you may be new to this particular type of analysis, and you may ultimately chalk it up to a "rookie" mistake.

In the case where the "outside" numbers are incorrect and your numbers are correct, you may have a different kind of unpleasant situation on your hands. In this scenario, you are the one who most recently introduced

---

[11] John Wooden with Steve Jamison, *Wooden: A Lifetime of Observations and Reflections On and Off the Court* (New York: McGraw-Hill, 1997).

the conflicting numbers, whether intentionally or unintentionally, and those "outside" numbers may have been the basis for some key decisions. Individuals associated with those outside numbers, if they are still around, will most likely be on the defensive. Inevitable questions like, "Do you mean all the numbers we've seen over the last year have been wrong?" is one nightmare question that comes to mind. The "outsiders," people who are on the receiving end of the numbers you are presenting, may put up quite a fight before conceding that their numbers are incorrect. An "outsider" can be someone who has typically been responsible for these numbers, but may have not kept things updated. They could be an executive who has pushed a strategic approach, based on these numbers.

Clearly, both situations carry some level of unpleasantness.

In the case where one party being incorrect can cause them real or perceived serious repercussions, they will sometimes opt for the face-saving resolution where they can claim both parties are correct, and that the two things being compared are not exactly the same. As you are the one presenting these numbers your best bet is to acknowledge the disconnect and indicate that you will try to resolve after the presentation, but keep things moving forward.

BOTH ARE CORRECT?

It is not uncommon for two seemingly similar metrics to disconnect and the main reason is that they are simply not calculated the same way. There are many examples of this. Most of these disconnects come down to a different definition of the metric itself or the time period for which it was calculated. In a marketing setting some examples include:

1. Did you use only current active customers, or are there inactive customers included as well?
2. Are you looking at the US, or the US plus Puerto Rico?
3. Are we looking at the same list of products for the market basket?
4. Is this over the last month, last year, most recent six or 12 months?
5. Are we using the same data sources?

Another more difficult problem to deal with is when two different analytical approaches yield different results, and both approaches seem valid. Resolving this requires a deeper understanding of both how the data was prepared/filtered as well as the methodological approaches. If there are assumptive differences, do these differences cause the main disconnect? In other words, if the assumptions were perfectly aligned, do both analyses draw the same conclusion? If so, you've isolated the main reason for the disconnect and are left with debating which assumption is more relevant to the problem at hand.

In many cases you have to undertake an exercise where you're trying to reconcile the different numbers. This reconciliation exercise essentially is going step-by-step through all the assumptions and programming code or queries to make sure you did everything correctly. At certain points you try to match up with expected numbers along the way, so you know you're remaining on the right track and can move forward.

The next step is to understand the reason for the disconnect. You may even learn something (the hard way). Continuing on with the process you will have done a more thorough check of your work. If you were on track all the way through, you can feel much more confident in your numbers.

Sometimes, you may not be able to resolve the differences in the time allotted. There's just too much to backtrack and each step may take a good deal of time. You can try to ask for more time if that's possible, but if not, you want to at least understand on your end if your approach to the data is sound later on.

YOU'RE BOTH WRONG

In the case where you're both wrong, it could be just a function of misunderstanding the question, assumptions, or you've made some errors along the way. The fact that the other person is also wrong may make you feel a little better. Ultimately, you want to make sure you're understanding the question being asked and are using the proper assumptions. If you do good checking as a habit as you're doing your analysis, your work will be more solid. Additionally, you won't have to backtrack as much when challenged. Also make sure that any time you can align to internal data trusted sources, you'll be on more solid ground.

Good quality control (QC) requires that you check your numbers every step of the way. Do basic checks like making sure the number of records in your file match with the expected number of records. Don't just assume that your programming code seems correct. Do numerical spot checks during your process. Ask questions if you're not sure of what those basic counts should be. Ask others in the know how many records should be on certain key files. You don't want to find out things like the correct number of customers is 10,000 and your file says 8,000. Find out why your file count is different.

As you discipline yourself and make this approach part of your general behavior, you'll find that you become much more proficient in the intricacies of the different databases. As a result, you'll also be more confident when challenged.

CHAPTER 11

THAT'S RIGHT, I WANT POWERPOINT SLIDES

After doing all the analysis and even informally conveying some of your findings, the next step is to pull all that hard work together and summarize it into some type of story. As an analyst, you may feel like you've done all the heavy lifting and it's time for someone else to take your results and present them. While each situation is different, my recommendation is to fight this feeling and to tie all your hard work together into the analysis summary story, which initially should come directly from you.

The most common currency used for final presentation summaries is the PowerPoint slide deck. (While you may prefer another type of presentation software, it is not critical with respect to the ensuing discussion.)

Putting together slides that tell your story, especially for the analyst, can sometimes be a challenge. You are now shifting gears into not only conveying how you pulled the data together and analyzed it, but concurrently having a good story flow. You want your slides to have a crisp and professional look to it, without overwhelming your audience. Additionally, you want to show compelling insights without being too technical.

The fact is that connecting with the viewer of your slides has a lot to do with who you are presenting to. Ideally, you want to present your work in person, so you can give context to what you're trying to say live, however, you may not always get the chance. As a result, your PowerPoint slides have to do the talking for you.

There are a few types of PowerPoint decks that I've generally seen in the business setting. The two I'd like to highlight are:

1. The PowerPoint deck that has anywhere from 20 to 200 slides trying to cover all areas.
2. The PowerPoint deck that is anywhere from 10 to under 20 slides that tries to cover some key points and puts forth a couple of key insights, with executive summary and next steps.

The first type of presentation is in a sense more of a document than it is a presentation. It is still popular in the business environment because executives like to have all the information to reference and can decide which areas of the deck they want to focus on. This deck usually requires a "pre-read," which gives the recipients time to digest the information prior to the actual live delivery of the presentation. Usually, on the day of the presentation the highest-ranking executive after some intros and maybe a slide or two in, may bark out something like, "Can we jump to slide 56? I have a real problem with what that's saying," just to get things rolling.

The second type of presentation is where I'm going to focus my attention.

In this presentation, I generally like to present the analysis as a story building to a conclusion. I've found it's always a good idea to let folks know how the presentation is going to flow by including an agenda slide.

Once I turn to the analysis at hand, I prefer to first state what the overall business objective is and the main question being asked. In other words, why is this analysis being done. For example, there's been a general lagging of sales across the country over some portion of time currently. I usually like to follow that with the project objective, which is going to be more of how you're going to look at the problem analytically, even getting into the data sources that are being used. From there I like to hit some of the key statistics and just reintroduce the numerical portion of what was observed. At that point I like to get right to the results and how I got there, and go right to the "whats," "whys," and "hows."

Showing things graphically is usually more powerful or even graphically coupled with tables.

You should close the presentation with some sort of executive summary as well as the "hows," which are the recommended actions you are proposing from the analysis as well as any follow-up activities that need to be done to continue to try to answer the question, if necessary. I also like to keep more detailed slides in backup, as supplemental slides, in case certain questions come up that folks might be interested in, but I'm not necessarily presenting directly as part of the story.

When I build these PowerPoint presentations there are number of things that I like to do. My main motto has been, Be paranoid in preparation, not in presentation. What I mean by that is I try to think of all the key questions that different people might ask, and then ask myself if I have thought them through. I have even asked people as I'm doing the analysis, "What are some concerns or questions you might have? Are there ways I can address them up front, especially if they may be in the audience?"

Presentations are never going to be perfect and you're going to get a lot of feedback, as well as follow-ups on certain findings. That's okay as long as you're putting out a good analysis and you're trying to answer the question. If you're thinking about the "whats," "whys," and "hows," you're usually in a good place to start and it also gets good conversations going.

Clearly every situation varies, and I'm not going to minimize the fact that there are timing issues in terms of what's available, how long it takes you to do analysis, how much time you've been given to pull the presentation together, what your boss wants, people in the room, and those who may not like some of the results you might be presenting. How to deal with all of this needs to be considered, but first I want to start with the basic structure.

There are other logistics I like to consider and usually like to make sure I've considered before presenting. It doesn't hurt to get feedback on how you're approaching the problem beforehand, as it may give you a different perspective on what you could or should be looking at. It is also a good idea to rehearse the presentation to see if it flows well and you're comfortable presenting it. You will find out as you start to discuss a particular slide, whether or not it's easy to get to the point you're trying to make.

Other logistics I like to consider is what room I'm presenting in. What is the tech in that room? Is it working? Is it possible for me to book the room for the half hour prior to the meeting so I can get set up? There's nothing more irritating and distracting than spending the first few minutes dealing with tech issues. Getting there early to make sure you're all set technically, as well as getting your energy and focus up works best. It also makes good use of the time you have, once the meeting starts. Printed backup copies are also good to have as people like to write notes on them, and they can go through them at their own speed.

At the end of the day, you are a salesperson for what you've found and what you're recommending. How persuasive is your analytic argument? Shoring up those areas is part of the paranoia portion of your preparation.

"Be paranoid in preparation, not in presentation."

During the slide-building process, I do my best to make sure that each slide is not too busy and gets to the point as soon as possible. One of the tests I have is to set up a slide that gets my meaning across to anyone in a few seconds. When you're on the receiving end of the presentation you don't want to work that hard to try to understand what the presenter is trying to tell you in the slide. Once you get past about six or seven seconds as the recipient, you start to get frustrated internally and you're asking yourself quietly, "What is the point of this slide? I'm trying to listen to the speaker and at the same time stare at the slide and try to figure out if there's a point in here somewhere." As the presenter, try to make sure that doesn't happen. You want your slides and your message to be clear.

As I mentioned, you don't want your slides to be too busy. I have seen too many analytical presentations where the focus is on jamming as much information and graphics onto a slide, while also trying to make it as artistically pleasing as possible. I always find it amusing when someone points out that they like the look of a certain slide deck but struggle to explain what the takeaway is of those really fancy slides.

In his book *PresentationZen*, Garr Reynolds says, "Slides are slides. Documents are documents. They aren't the same thing."[12] He calls the merging of the two a "slideument." This slideument is an attempt to get all the information compiled into one slide, but the overall visuals are extremely busy and difficult to assimilate.

I'm also a big fan of what's sometimes called "slide headlining." It's pretty self-explanatory—your title should tell you what the headline of the slide is in as few words as possible. Having the title say something like "Monthly Sales" with a graphic that shows the monthly sales leads to the user having to figure out the point of this slide. Even if it's a simple review of the data, it's still a good idea to highlight some summary of the sales. Is it growing by a certain percent, declining by a certain percent, is it following a norm, or is it departing from the norm? Capture that in the headline. If you're showing a distribution by state, putting the list in alphabetical order by state is probably not as visually informative. It might be better to rank from either highest to lowest or lowest to highest, whether in a table or graphically so that the viewer can easily tell where most of the business is coming from, or areas that do not generate much business. It may generate an interesting discussion as to the whys of certain patterns. You might want to think about those highs and lows in advance, so you're ready for those "why" questions.

As I'm going through any particular slide during the paranoia stage, I like to ask myself the question, "So what?" This "So what?" question test is also recommended by Reynolds in *PresentationZen*.[13] That question gets me thinking about why I think this particular slide is important to show. This technique gets me more focused on what the key takeaways are from the analysis. It also helps me decide whether the information and takeaway message is slide-worthy.

---

[12] Garr Reynolds, *PresentationZen: Simple Ideas for Presentation Design and Delivery* (Berkeley, CA: New Riders, 2011).

[13] Renolds, *PresentationZen*.

Also, for those who have more advanced analytic skills, you don't want to parrot too much technical jargon. Don't assume your audience knows about the advanced statistical method you used. I've seen individuals who always highlight their PhD status in the presentation title (for internal company presentations). In many cases that's fine, but sometimes citing their degree is kind of a preemptive reminder that you should expect that their conclusions, no matter how unclear, need to be adopted, as their credentials are impeccable.

For example, let's say you were presenting a particular forecast for a particular product's sales in the coming year. You've been asked to show how you came up with your choice of forecast. One approach might be to show more of the visual motivation for how you've arrived at your forecast line.

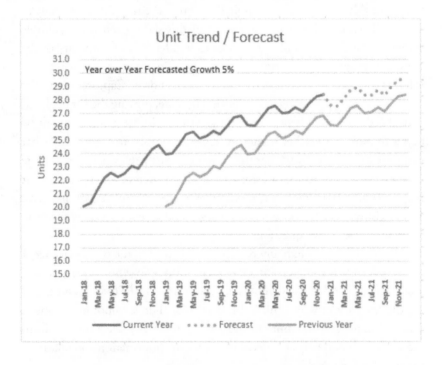

The second approach would be to show in tabular format the sales for the most recent years and the forecast number for the upcoming year. In explaining how you came up with the number, you point out that you've run a Box–Jenkins times series autoregressive, moving average model with certain AR and MA parameters, as well as a Winter's model.[14] Both approaches had a good fit, are in close agreement, and therefore the forecast number for next year should be solid.

Units	Y2018	Y2019	Y2020	Y2021E	Est. Growth
Actuals	270.00	305.04	326.86		
Box-Jenkins				351.38	8%
Winters				350.39	7%
Standard				342.78	5%

The first chart is much easier to follow and understand. The second chart uses more advanced statistical techniques. The year over year percentage growth differences may not seem large, but the dollars associated with those differences may indeed be sizable.

As a presenter you need to find ways to show your results at a more digestible level. Saying something like, "The advanced model shows that X is true," doesn't make folks feel they understand why. They need to see more evidence. A detective saying that their new advanced method points to a certain individual as the guilty party isn't enough.

Sophisticated methods that are difficult to explain, especially for those not as technical, are called "black boxes." In cases like this there is this dynamic where the advanced analytic presenter is saying, "It's hard to explain, but trust me, the method is well known, and well supported in the literature." This is not very comforting to the person making the business decisions. In addition, you don't want to make your audience feel dumb. ("This is too advanced for me to explain to you.") They are going to need some more non-black-box details.

Now, I'm not saying you're going to have all the answers, but you want to be in command of what the analysis showed you. You may also have open-ended results. For example, you're seeing a pattern. You've tried to

---

[14] "The Box-Jenkins Method," NCSS Statistical Software, accessed March 1, 2021, https://ncss-wpengine.netdna-ssl.com/wp-content/themes/ncss/pdf/Procedures/NCSS/The_Box-Jenkins_Method.pdf.

determine what you think might be going on, but you're opening it up for feedback. This may create a fruitful discussion that may lead somewhere, but use this type of approach sparingly. At the end of the presentation, you want to have some sort of executive summary of what you found and potential next steps.

As you're presenting, you also want to have access to a place where you could jot down feedback, or ideally if a colleague can help you out, they can keep track of the questions that come up so that you're not too distracted.

Either way you want to make sure to capture all that feedback. It will give you a better understanding of how different individuals are thinking. This will most certainly help you in the long run.

Having said all this, and putting you in a place where you thought through all the analytics, logistics, and some do's and don'ts of the presentation, there is one dynamic out of your control for which you have to be prepared. As much as I'm a big fan of building a story and pacing the presentation, the reality is that you may not get past your first two or three slides. Someone will have a reaction to something in one of your slides and/or one of the higher-ranking participants wants to take the discussion deeper into one of the areas you mentioned. As a result, this departure will probably interrupt your planned flow. Don't let this throw you, because it's very likely to happen. You have to move with that flow, and not be too frustrated with the presentation story derailment. Once that departure discussion has resolved, calmly try to return to your key messages.

One other takeaway from this is that you want to get to the main point of your presentation as quickly as possible. If there's too much presentation story buildup, you might not get there. Keep in mind that as much as we all may like a story, most of us are running from meeting to meeting, and want to get to the point. This is especially true for higher-level executives.

There are also other presentation types that generate a lot of energy. One of those types is known as Pecha Kucha.[15] Essentially this presentation type requires to presenter to go through 20 slides in 20 seconds. As a result the entire presentation takes six minutes and 40 seconds. These can be quite fun and challenging to build. While there may be some exceptions in certain organizations, I've found that most executives do not want to

---

[15] Reynolds, *PresentationZen*, 41.

speed through the presentation, especially when they want to digest and dig into the results of an analysis.

Overall, you want to capture your summarized big analytic findings, for the most part, in PowerPoint slides. When final presentations are made, they generally end up in slide format (whether they are .pptx or .pdf). As an analyst, you want to make sure those findings are clear, concise, and understandable. You also want to get to your points quickly.

While it may seem painful at times to "build another slide," it's usually worth the trouble. You may even be surprised every so often that one of your slides could end up as part of a deck presented to a large audience.

CHAPTER 12

THE PRIVATE EYE
OF THE BEHOLDER

Sometimes as an analyst, you are so focused on the data and making sure that you've captured things correctly, that you might not realize that presenting certain information unfettered might put certain individuals in an uncomfortable position. It might even make them angry.

To illustrate this, let's pick a simple sports example. The head coach of the team has been there for one full season and it is now early into her second season. The team was in fifth place in a division of six teams prior to the coach arriving. In the coach's first season, the team again finished in fifth place. Early into the coach's second season the team has been struggling.

An analyst has been asked to do some analysis to help find some insights in the data. The analyst starts the presentation with a slide that shows performance history and current trends. Based on the current trends the analyst points out what everyone in the room already knows all too well. The season did not get off to a good start. Innocently, the analyst leads with this visual in front of the coach, even showing a trend line of fifth place. This is not something they want to be reminded of. The analysis looks correct, but pointing out something that's obvious and unpleasant to someone, especially a high-ranking someone, is not a good idea. In this case, unless there's something really helpful that the analyst is going to show very quickly, the presentation may not last past that first two slides, and that could be the last time the analyst is invited to present again.

This example may seem unrealistic, but situations like this happen all the time. In fact, the analyst may be oblivious to what just happened. To them, they were just presenting the data. Unfortunately for them, they picked at a sensitive wound, and they didn't even know it. Even worse, no one will tell them at the meeting, with, most likely, the exception of their boss, who's probably regretting not looking over the presentation in advance. I want to be clear that I'm not asking for unpleasant data to be suppressed, but to be presented with care.

In the example of the sports team in fifth place, dedicating a slide to showing the history and *trending* the current year might be a little too much. The purpose was to conduct an analysis that could show how to improve the current situation. Instead of leading with an entire slide dedicated to the poor performance history and current trend, an alternative approach might be to point out that while the team was off to a slow start this year, there are some encouraging metrics and potentially opportunities. Teams in a similar situation in the past who have turned things around did X, Y, and Z as an example. Then go into the findings.

"A common criticism of analytic folks is that they have no awareness beyond the numbers they present and what those numbers may indicate in terms of how individuals will react."

With all the types of information you're presenting, the analyst has to realize that any slide can and will create some type of reaction. Each individual set of private eyes is processing the results you're showing differently. Their first reaction is to understand what you're showing. Their next reaction:

1. Interests them so they want to learn more.
2. Lines up with their beliefs, so they're in agreement.

3. Bores them.
4. Does not line up with their beliefs and it might upset them.
5. Puts them on the defensive.

The first two reactions are obviously positive and those who are react-ing to what you're showing in this way will want to hear more. Not every slide will elicit positive or engaged reactions, and that's okay too. The third reaction of not being very interested in a particular slide may be fine, but if this reaction is what a certain individual is experiencing through a number of consecutive slides, then you've probably lost them. You will recognize them as their smartphone will most likely become the visual they'll be following.

The ones to be most attuned to are the last two reactions. You're pre-senting something that conflicts with held beliefs or you're putting them directly or indirectly on the defensive.

Let's take reaction 4. You're presenting something that challenges cer-tain individual beliefs. Are you aware that they might disagree? If so, you should ask yourself a few questions:

1. Is the result you're proposing critical to your analysis?
2. Is it worth it to provoke this reaction during the presentation?
3. Who are the people who might disagree?

The first question is important. If the result is not critical to your anal-ysis, then it's probably not worth putting it out there just to tick off folks. If the result is important to your analysis, then you want to fully under-stand where that disagreement comes from. This may help you think of a better, less confrontational way to make your ultimate analytical point.

One example that comes to mind is around something I've observed in a few industries, which I'll refer to as "summer weakness." For certain products, the demand during the summer wanes, as people are on vaca-tion, may not be eyeballing as much TV advertising, and/or just aren't thinking about the need for your type of product in the summer.

The analyst gets up and presents expected demand by quarter and builds in the summer weakness component. This chart starts a heated conversation around whether that summer lull is really going to happen. "If we believe that, then our sales for the second half of the year look off," someone might say. In addition, some people in the meeting might question whether the summer advertising spend makes sense. From the analyst's standpoint, the built in "summer weakness" is justified because it happens every year. Others may feel that if the summer strategic and tactical efforts are handled correctly, the summer lull won't happen.

Finally, if one of the higher-ranking people in the meeting, or even your boss, is clearly not going to like what you're putting out there as a recommendation, it is not a good idea to put that in front of them. For example, if you do choose to pursue this path and you're wrong, you've struck out on two fronts: you've not only irritated another influential individual, but you've also unnecessarily challenged their opinion. If you're correct, you may win the argument, but the other party will most likely see you as a threat and/or hostile party. Depending on their position they could limit you in the future (without you even knowing it).

I once heard it said that "being right is overrated." This is one of those cases. It is always a tough situation, but you have to resist the urge to take on this battle directly and publicly. If at some point in the future your position is vindicated, you want to take that victory lap privately.

Simply being aware of certain points of view beforehand is important. If you are aware of this situation up-front, it's a good idea to get some guidance from your boss and possibly others who can be of assistance. Sometimes you may be able to ask one of the folks who might have concerns directly (in advance) about how you can broach the subject, so that you're both happy with the way the information can be shared.

In cases where you didn't know about an individual's disagreement, then you might get a good challenge during the presentation. Always be respectful of the question and explain how you came to your conclusion. You may end up agreeing to disagree.

The last reaction is when an individual is on the defensive, likely due to something performance-based that is being displayed in the slide. This is quite common when slides on different sales areas, regions, or territories are summarized in a total sales force picture. They may display top-bottom sales volume, market share, or possibly most recent growth. You, as the analyst, might want to show some interesting patterns nationally, but the different sales leaders in those specific geographies are looking at their numbers and wondering if they're going to be put on the spot about being toward the bottom on one of those metrics. While sales leaders are used to seeing these types of summaries and are usually aware of the numbers, they definitely don't want the reminders when they're not in a good place on the list.

I recall an experience where I had a visual (a standard four-quadrant bubble chart) of market share and market share change where the quadrants were separated by the overall market share for the nation and overall market share change for the nation. This indicated where the different regions stood with respect to the national averages. The bubbles themselves represented the individual regions. If you fell in the top right quadrant your region was ahead of both national averages. If you fell in the bottom left quadrant your region was below both national averages.

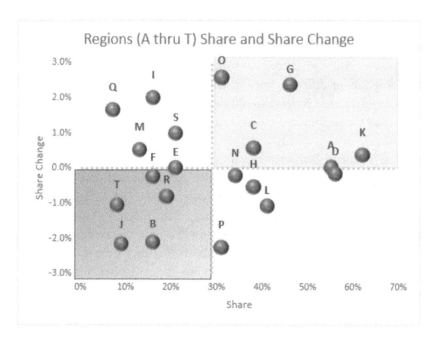

As the original request for the analysis was to look for national as well as regional patterns, I didn't give too much thought to this bubble-chart visual. As it turned out, a very high-ranking executive saw this chart and loved it. They wanted to see this for every brand on a weekly basis.

These meetings were scheduled every Friday. In fact, since these were one of the KPIs we now were tracking, we used to call those Fridays "KPI Fridays." Needless to say, the regional heads on that day did not say TGIF.

The high-ranking executive would typically show up at these meetings. When someone's region was at the top right, they were very proud as they were asked to share with the others on the call what was working for them. Of course, those on the bottom left would have to speak to what might be challenging in their area. The leader assured those with challenges that they were not being called out negatively. The purpose of the meeting was to understand what they were seeing and was there anything that we as a team could assist with.

While they were given those assurances, they dreaded being in the bottom left, and it motivated them to get out of that quadrant. One person asked me what it would take to move their bubble out of that quadrant. While I found the request amusing and knew it was only half-serious; I didn't entertain it.

When I look back on that experience, I have to say that the field leadership never really gave me a hard time about it, as they were more used to seeing lots of different ways to rank their regions. What I did learn from the experience is that I would think through some of the underlying metrics at the regional level that could be causing those differences (i.e., the "why").

I also realized that what was to me a simple graphic could "get legs" and become something you didn't quite expect. In addition, that slide could potentially make some folks defensive. Some would argue that it did motivate stronger focus (which it did). As an analyst, you want to offer insight on what could be done to reverse a disappointing trend.

A common criticism of analytic folks is that they have no awareness beyond the numbers they present and what those numbers may indicate in terms of how individuals will react. When building presentations make sure you get some feedback beforehand of what you might be showing and recommending. You should run things by your boss as well as others who have some responsibility for the data you're showing in advance. If they have some issue, it's better to find out privately versus publicly. They will appreciate the heads-up and be even more appreciative if you can adapt your slides so that you're both comfortable with the result.

In short, a seasoned analyst learns to be more than just about the numbers. They need to be keenly aware and to be able to respond to specific meeting dynamics before and during the presentation.

CHAPTER 13

IT'S NOT PERSONAL, IT'S ANALYTICAL

In one of the many memorable scenes in the 1972 movie *The Godfather*, the character Michael Corleone proposes a way to retaliate for a murder attempt on his father. He is accused of taking things too personally. He presses his point and insists to his brother Sonny, "It's not personal, Sonny. It's strictly business."[16]

While the stakes are clearly not as dire, analysts are quite often caught in situations where they are presenting results that might favor one commonly held point of view over an alternative popular point of view. Simply by presenting those results, those individuals whose point of view the analysis does not favor are usually not very happy with this. They may even take it personally, quietly thinking, "Why are you siding with them?"

As an analyst, every time you are displaying results and/or focusing on a certain insight you've found from your analysis, someone or some group of people in the organization may feel some responsibility for those results, good or bad. If the results are good, they are happy to take the credit, but if the results are not so good, they will also be happy to avert their eyes to

---

[16] *The Godfather*, directed by Francis Ford Coppola (Paramount Pictures, 1972).

the individuals who they believe are responsible for addressing why those results are what they are.

As mentioned in Chapter 12, an analyst has to convey what the data is saying, but at the same time realize that sometimes the insights you believe you've found from the data may put others on the defensive.

When channeling the analytic detective spirit, you generally want to follow the clues, figure out the puzzle, and solve the (statistical) crime. You're also supporting clients and you want to keep them happy. What if the solution to the puzzle won't make your client happy? I want to be clear here, that I'm not advocating for suppressing actual data. What I am saying is that you, as an analyst, will have to work out the best way to show that data (e.g., the fifth-place sports team). This can be very challenging as the path to getting to common ground in certain situations can be quite painful, time consuming, and very difficult for the analyst to navigate.

When your boss or a key client is a "true believer" about a certain trend or metric, you will most likely have to go along, but at the same time make sure to maintain your analytic integrity.

Trusted analytic folks or groups are typically put in the position where they might be unwittingly judging how decisions should be made going forward, based on their analysis alone. (Hey, you can't argue with the data.)

WHAT'S THE ROI?

One of the more challenging and potentially hazardous requests an analyst gets is captured in a simple question: "What's the ROI of a particular tactic or effort?" Simply stated, does the initial investment pay off? Seems like an innocuous question, but there are a couple potential minefields along the way.

The basic concept of getting a return for your investment is nothing new, however the acronym seems to have been formalized back in the 1920s at DuPont by Donaldson Brown.[17]

ROI is either quoted as a ratio or a percent. If you invested $X and your return was $Y, your ROI would be quoted as either

ROI Ratio: Y/X : 1,

---

[17] Dale L. Flesher and Gary John Previts, "Donaldson Brown (1885-1965): The Power of an Individual and His Ideas Over Time," *The Accounting Historians Journal* 40, Iss. 1, Article 5 (2013), https://egrove.olemiss.edu/aah_journal/vol40/iss1/5.

OR

ROI Percent: $(Y/X - 1)*100\%$

For example, if you invested $100 and your return was $150, your ROI Ratio would be 150/100:1 which is 1.5:1 or your ROI percent would be (150/100-1)*100% which is a 50% return.

If I stick with the ROI Ratio then 1:1 is called breakeven. Anything > 1:1 is considered a positive ROI and <1:1 is considered a negative ROI.

Depending on where you work, ROI is either quoted as the ":1" ratio or as the positive/negative percent.

There are also many cousins of the ROI metric that are used for different situations. Examples include ROE (Return on Equity), ROA (Return on Assets), ROS (Return on Sales), ROIC (Return on Investment Capital), EBITA (Earnings Before Income Taxes and Amortization), and a number of other financial metrics. As an analyst, you want to find out which financial metrics are used for analyses you might get involved in. For the purpose of this discussion, I will stick with ROI.

What makes the ROI question tricky is that there is someone on the other end of that result. In other words, when you declare that some initial investment generated a certain ROI, there is a person or a group of people who are associated with that investment recommendation either directly or indirectly.

If the result is that the investment has a positive ROI (or exceeds some ROI threshold), then usually everyone will be happy. If the ROI is negative (or does not exceed some ROI threshold), then folks will be unhappy.

This feeling of happy or unhappy, based on ROI, might be just a little deeper on the unhappy side. The person attached to a less than acceptable ROI tactic will most likely not accept those results. They are sure to claim that something must have been done incorrectly. There's a little bit more at stake for them, and they're taking your analysis a little personally.

On the happy side, if the ROI is positive, they'll just love what you've done with the analysis, and they'll laud your analytic skills.

Which situation would you prefer to experience? Well, as much as you'd like to be part of the positive ROI experience, your job is to treat the exercise in an unbiased manner. That's easy to say, but the reality is that the person who wants to see your results first, usually has a conflict of interest.

Ideally, the best way to try to assess whether a tactic increases sales is to set up test and control cells where each cell is as similar as possible across a variety of attributes. The test cell is then exposed to the tactic and the control cell is not exposed to the tactic. The basic idea is that if you're able control for other factors, then the increase in sales of the test versus control is most likely due to the tactic ("treatment") itself.

For example, we want to test a particular marketing effort. If we were able to deploy the effort in a part of the country and not deploy that effort in a similar part of the country, we could assess whether the effort worked. This "control group" portion of the country would share a similar profile and similar sales performance compared to the "test group" prior to the deployment of the marketing effort. Once the marketing effort is deployed, we could track whether there is some gap in trend when comparing the test versus control groups.

Let's say we're using Designated Marketing Areas (DMA's) for the geographical groups. We selected test and control DMAs that were very similar in profile and performance.

For example, these areas have similar demographics: average age, median income, number of active customers, and potential strong prospects.

When plotting the test versus control sales chart we would also plot the test-control "gap." Taking a technique from quality control measurement, we could construct what is known as a Shewhart chart. The Shewhart chart, which can be represented as a plot through time, looks to determine whether a process is performing as expected (i.e., "in-control") or is outside the control bounds.

For this example, we could plot the test-control DMA gap each week. Let's assume we see that there is no underlying trend, and that the mean gap is 0.03 and the standard deviation is approx. 0.34. The Shewhart chart would plot the time series, and would have lower and upper control bounds. Given that we would expect the test to outperform the control, we would be more focused on a (one-sided) upper control limit. These bounds are typically set at three standard deviations, and any gap exceeding three x 0.34 units (+ or -) would be considered out of control. For the one-sided example you could set the upper control at a less stringent two standard deviations.[18] A working marketing effort would equate to an "out-of-control" condition (i.e., the gap greater than the upper control limit). This is a

---

[18] Christopher .J Wild and George A.F. Seber, *Chance Encounters: A First Course in Data Analysis and Inference* (Hoboken, NJ: Wiley, 2000), Chapter 13.

method I've used for many years and like to call the "trend-gap approach," as you want to see a gap trend break. If you're able to set up an in-market experiment like this up-front, the results once the marketing tactic is deployed will speak for itself.

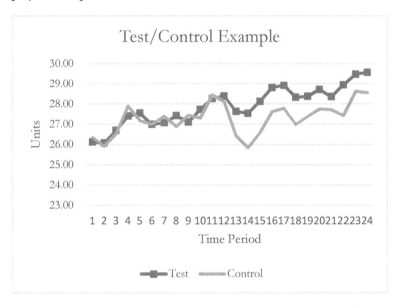

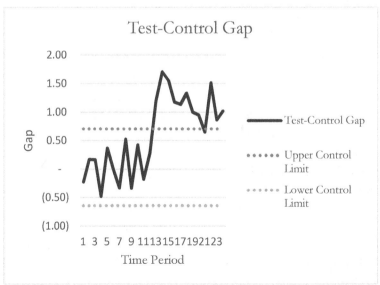

While this may sound great, businesses often don't have the patience for testing programs and tactical approaches. They don't like to purposely hold out any customers from potential new business, so that they can scientifically test whether the approach works.

The best-case scenario is that you can design these test/control groups up front and then track them to see whether the exposed-to-tactic group performs better versus the control. This is usually the ideal situation, as you can argue over the test/control group dynamics and get everyone to align before the data comes in. Once the data comes in, you, as an analyst, can feel less pressure with the approach should the results not be as strong as expected.

The more common situation is that the tactic was already deployed and you, as an analyst, have been being asked to assess the ROI after the fact. You can try to retreat to the position that to properly assess ROI there should have been an upfront attempt at a randomized test/control group. While you may be correct, that position is not going to satisfy those who are asking. They would agree that you're correct, but they will want you to come up with some alternative way to give some "directional" guidance.

In cases like these you want to find out first if the effort was somewhat localized (i.e., only delivered to certain areas or segment types). Second, for those areas and/or segments that didn't get exposed to the effort, is that pool of individuals adequate enough to construct a (after the fact) control, sometimes referred to as a "pseudo-control?" The basic idea would be to take the localized group and then match on a few variable criteria prior to the campaign launch. The test group and control group would look very similar in the pre-campaign launch period. In the post-campaign launch period, the increase in sales versus expected sales could be accumulated and a running ROI could be constructed.

Using the first example, we notice that the cumulative gap in the pre-period is approximately 0. Once the campaign is launched you observe cumulative sales after four weeks to be around $5,500, around eight weeks, you observe $10,000 cumulatively, and at 11 weeks you observe approximately $13,000 (and that has seemed to be staying around $13,000-$14,000). If you spent $10,000 on the effort by week 11, the straight ROI would be approximately 1.3:1 – 1.4:1. (With carryover, the ROI may get to 1.5.)

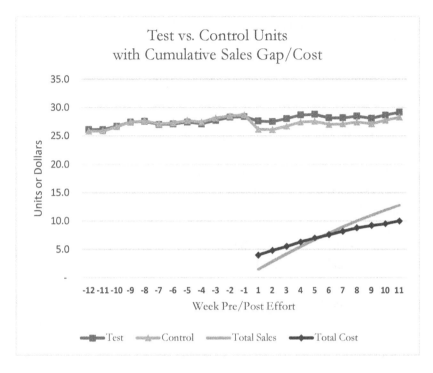

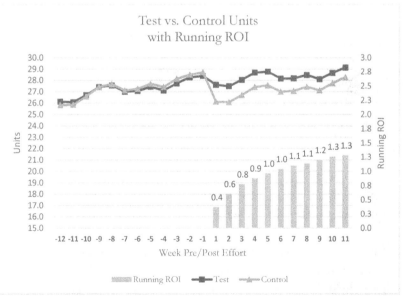

To further confound your ROI challenge, you find out that there is some internal belief at the company that if a tactic doesn't generate at least a 2:1 ROI, it's not worth continuing.

When an analyst asks around about where the 2:1 ROI came from, the conversation might go as follows:

Analyst: "Where's does the 2:1 benchmark come from?"

Marketer: "That's what's generally been observed for successful tactics."

Analyst: "How were the computations done?"

Marketer: "Usually the outside company that helped us deploy the tactic also puts the ROI analysis together. Having said that, our management wants more of an internal assessment of ROI."

Translation: management may not be a big believer in some of the ROIs they've seen in the past. They tend to believe that all the ROIs seem to look too good to be true. In fact, I've heard one executive say, "I have yet to see an ROI I didn't like. I'm a little skeptical."

Personally, I have found these situations to be common:

- Up-front test/control may not be an option.
- Management is suggesting some ROI inflation.
- Marketing is nervous that you might find an unacceptable ROI.

"What makes the ROI question tricky is that there is someone on the other end of that result."

At the risk of referencing a second organized crime movie in the same chapter, there's a scene in *Goodfellas* that always comes to mind when I hear, "What's the ROI of that effort?"

In the film, the characters Jimmy and Henry have just pulled off the big Lufthansa heist. Jimmy is becoming more annoyed with one of the other individuals named Morrie, who was also involved. He's concerned that Morrie talks too much and may get them arrested. While Jimmy is walking down the street with Henry, he asks Henry if he thinks Morrie told his wife about the heist. The screen freezes and Henry narrates, "That's when I knew Jimmy was gonna whack Morrie. That's how it happens. That's how fast it takes for a guy to get whacked."[19]

I always feel that the minute someone in upper management is asking about the ROI of something, they're usually questioning whether that tactic should get whacked.

Sitting in the analyst seat, you've got a challenging task.

One critical detail about the ROI question is what time period are we talking about? The tactic may work, but it doesn't generate returns overnight. This can be overlooked if the analyst isn't asked about it up front or early on.

The first thing to consider for ROI analysis is to see what internal approaches have been used in the past. Is this the very first time that someone is asking how to measure internally? If not, try to find out what has been done before. Were folks accepting of that approach? Does it seem like a sound way to measure the performance? If so, you're not reinventing a whole new approach, and may have an easier time referencing.

In the absence of being able to create standard randomized test/control groups, are there ways that you can create and/or reference what is sometimes referred to as a "pseudo-control group?" With a pseudo-control group, you're trying to make the case that this holdout group is not perfectly designed up-front, but may serve the purpose of getting some sort of baseline estimate. For example, you have top customers in the Southwest part of the country. In the past a particular campaign was rolled out to those top customers, but every single one of those top customers was exposed to it. As a result, there is no control pool in that area to compare to. You might find that there is an area of the country that shares very similar dynamics to the tested area but was not exposed to the campaign. Can you use top customers from that area as a "pseudo-control"? If that's acceptable, you could track differences between the two groups, using the pseudo-control as a baseline for your ROI calculations.

A third approach in the absence of being able to create some type of control or baseline might be to model the impact of different levels of investment, if available, and estimate ROI through the final model that was built. This is sometimes difficult to present as you may have difficultly

---

[19] *Goodfellas*, directed by Martin Scorsese (Warner Bros., 1990).

convincing folks that the model is really capturing ROI to their satisfaction, or they just can't really follow the model from investment to return. Conversely, they just might not buy some of the model assumptions, which when varied slightly, swing ROI from positive to negative.

There are a couple of other things to be careful about when comparing test versus control (or "pseudo-control"). I have seen folks present the dynamics of both groups and show you that they share very similar attributes prior to the tactic being applied to the test group. For example, you'll be told that the average ages are the same, the percent of customers within the top states is similar, and, most importantly, the groups account for around the same amount of business. All things look aligned. The results show that the test group, while aligned with the control group in the time period prior to the tactic launch, saw a 28 percent increase in sales in the post-tactic launch period, compared to the control which saw a decline in sales of 8 percent.

Metrics	Test	Control
New York Percent	22%	23%
California Percent	45%	43%
Florida Percent	14%	15%
Average Age	32.3	31.4
Pre-Period Units	28.7	28.8
Post-Period Units	36.9	26.4
Lift Post vs. Pre Period	28%	(8%)

The only thing that wasn't mentioned was trend: Upon further inspection it's clear that the trajectories of both test and control were quite different in the pre-period.

The bottom line is that there was momentum in the pre-period for the test group that was quite different from the control group. Based on this chart it is almost a given that you would have seen a difference regardless of any tactic. This visual is lost when the results are presented in tabular form.

In short, don't forget to control for trend.

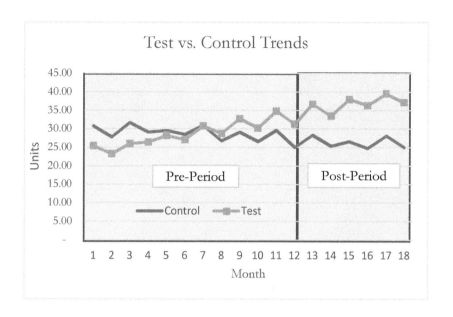

Overall, ROI questions can be very challenging. As you become more experienced as an analyst, you'll get better at navigating the potentially choppy waters of ROI analysis. Some ROI exercises will be straightforward, others may require some creative thinking. Offer different approaches. Try to get your boss to ride with you on any approach you choose, as you may find that you don't necessarily want to go it alone with these types of analyses.

CHAPTER 14

THE ANALYTIC INFORMATION BLINDSIDE

One of the more complex situations an analyst is confronted with usually starts with an e-mail or some type of communication of analytic information that seems on its face to be no big deal at all. What ensues can turn into quite a big deal for certain individuals who either weren't part of the initial communication and/or were unhappy that certain information went out without having been discussed with them first. This is what I refer to as the Analytic Information Blindside.

What makes it complicated is that you need to have good social awareness, business instinct, basic understanding of the company culture/structure, and a certain amount of Emotional Intelligence (EQ). Those qualities are not usually covered in the analytics handbook, but Daniel Goleman posits EQ as the primary indicator of job performance in his book *Working with Emotional Intelligence.*[20]

Here are some examples of situations an analyst might be confronted with. These examples all revolve specifically around the transmission and/or communication of database-oriented results.

---

[20] Daniel Goleman, *Working with Emotional Intelligence* (New York: Bantam, 2000).

Example 1: Your boss calls you live from a meeting they're having with their boss. "Hey, what's happening with the X and Y metric? Why do you think that Y is lower right now?" You give your boss what you believe to be the reason. His boss then confronts the head of group responsible for the Y metric, live. They're unaware. After the meeting that group head chews out their director, who then calls you and wants to know who gave them this idea without going through them?

Example 2: High ranking executive in the elevator. They recognize you and ask what you think about the latest data. Later that day your boss contacts you about the conversation you had, as they were asked about something you mentioned.

Example 3: Your boss's boss (or someone higher) contacts you directly about something they're working on. They want some specific summaries on some of the most recent data that was released.

Example 4: Your boss, who's in charge of analytics, has been asked to assess performance first thing Monday morning across the portfolio. It's Saturday and they're sorry to bother you, but you work on two of those brands for internal clients. They need some analytic talking points and comparisons.

Example 5: You're asked to present to your boss's boss and one level above them. Your boss will be present at this meeting. You are working hard to get everything done. You send the slides out to your boss only shortly before the meeting and they have not had a chance to review what you've put together.

Example 6: You send an analysis over to your client who forwards this to their boss. During a review later in the day, which your analytics boss is attending, your client's boss asks your boss questions about your analysis. Your boss hasn't seen it yet.

Example 7: Your boss is asked to assess the performance of a certain campaign internally. They delegate this work to you. You have the results. Your client finds out only after your boss presents those numbers.

Example 8: Your client is on vacation. You're getting the questions they would be getting directly while they're away. There is a lot of urgency to get this information out.

• • •

All of these examples have one component that's similar: someone who has some direct or indirect responsibility for understanding the results that were communicated to other key individuals was not made aware of those results themselves in advance.

Each of these situations are very dependent on the information that was shared. With most of these potential blindside scenarios, the analyst usually wanted nothing more than to just be responsive. Having said that, each example doesn't have perfect answers, but there are some basic tenets that you should follow as an analyst.

First and foremost, make sure your boss is clued into information you've either communicated verbally or sent out electronically. This is especially important if their boss went to you directly for some information. (The elevator conservation between you and your boss's boss would be a good example of informing your boss, so they are aware.) Now you might be saying, I don't need to cc my boss on *everything*, especially if it's information they're already aware of. That might be the case and you could be correct. Your boss might even reinforce that sentiment and indicate that they don't need to be cc'd on every e-mail. This is really at your discretion and judgment.

What I've found is that I like to err on the safe side. On one end the boss may be saying, "You don't need to copy me on everything" until that moment when they're asking you, "Why didn't you copy me on that thing?"

There are unfortunately other situations where a requestor asks you for information, and their understanding is that information is for their eyes only. By looping in others (even your boss), they feel that some confidence has been betrayed. They were having a 1:1 conversation with you, and now you've brought others into the conversation. The worst part is that you just forwarded the entire thread of back-and-forth e-mails between you and them, and they're now mortified that you just hit the forward button to others.

THE ANALYTIC
BLINDSIDE

In this situation I would tend to agree with the requestor about forwarding the chain without their consent. With respect to the information itself, you would need to make the call if the information is important for your boss to see. If so, it's better to let the requestor know that you'd like to share the analytic information with your boss. In addition, you should start a brand-new e-mail that doesn't have the whole e-mail thread. You could let your boss know what the key information is, and cc the requestor. The other subtle dynamic is that you're showing respect for your requestor's conversational privacy and that is usually appreciated and trusted.

Knee-jerk thread forwarding to everyone isn't always received well, and could cause some real problems, especially when there is some dicey commentary in the thread, and the forwarder didn't look at it really carefully. Some might edit out anything that looks a little compromising and forward relevant information. This might work, but again the requestor may not like the knee-jerk forwarding.

What's important to realize as an analyst is that you have access to information that others may not have the skills to summarize. You want to answer questions that are posed, but at the same time give a second thought to what those results might indicate. Maybe the results you're putting together are a big deal, and maybe they're not. Will they get a reaction that might not be too pleasant? Could you be caught in the middle of some executive argument, as your results might clearly favor one side? Either way you have to deliver those results, but also think for yourself what those results might mean.

In a scene from the 1992 film *Glengarry Glen Ross*, Al Pacino's salesman character, Ricky Roma, is trying to assure a customer he need not worry, and should he choose to do so, he has plenty of time to reconsider canceling a deal and stopping a check. Trying to distract the customer, Roma's intentions are really subterfuge. He hopes that a three-day clock will run out and the customer won't be able to cancel the check. When that clock runs out, Roma will make money ($6,000) on the deal. One of the managers, thinking he is being helpful, tells the customer the check was deposited. The customer, visibly upset by this, leaves. We know based on Roma's reaction the deal will be cancelled. Roma's plan and deal have now been ruined. The manager was not aware of what Roma was trying to do.

Roma then lambasts this manager and says to him, "You never open your mouth, till you know what the shot is."[21]

This is a pretty raw example, but it does point out that you might have information whether correct or not, that might create a certain reaction. You could have inadvertently derailed someone, something they were working on, or blew up a theory they've been espousing.

Understanding what your results can mean is important. Again, I'm not recommending you suppress those results, but make sure you keep those closest to those results informed, whenever possible.

If you've accidentally or unavoidably communicated something others wanted to know about first, do your best to make those connections as soon as possible. It can be very tricky. If you're unsure of what to do, reach out to colleagues or your boss first and ask for guidance on how to handle certain communications.

If you have results of an analysis and have put together the summary, take an extra moment to think through if you should be keeping someone else in the loop before you hit the send button. You may have been so caught up in getting those results before some sort of deadline, that you didn't have a chance to think through the implications of sending. It's worth the extra time to think about any potential unintended consequences that could put you in hot water. Sometimes it's unavoidable. In those cases, you have to choose the lesser of two evils. Again, if your boss and/or colleagues can help you, don't hesitate to ask for their guidance.

As an analyst, you will definitely find yourself in situations where not only do you have to rush to do the analysis, but you will also have to conduct a reconnaissance mission to make sure you've ensured your "safety," even though you didn't start the fire. While these are not analytic skills, you need to hone them.

You might have done a great analysis. You want to make sure you're remembered for that work, and not for screwing up the communication path for those results.

---

[21] *Glengarry Glen Ross*, directed by James Foley (New Line Cinema, 1992).

~

CHAPTER 15

ARTIFICIAL INTELLIGENCE OR OFFICIAL INTELLIGENCE

At some point during your analytic journey, trying to provide valuable and actionable analytic insights to your customers, it's inevitable that one of these customers will entertain the idea of bringing in outside (third-party) analytics. The objective would be to send them all of the relevant internal data that your company compiles and any work you or your team have put together in order to run this data through their more sophisticated analytic or artificial intelligence software.

This request is usually posed under the auspices that the analytics group hasn't really dug deep enough into the company's data and that there must be a plethora of great insights that can only be unlocked through some AI software package or technology.

From the internal analytics group's standpoint, they usually find out about this initiative once it's already in motion. At that point the analytics group is either brought in to align with the initiative or they may not be very much involved at all. In both cases they are left wondering what happened. They feel as if they haven't been told what in fact they had been missing up to this point. What were the questions that they weren't answering? Unless the analytics team was part of the initial decision to get outside help, they will generally find this demotivating, not to mention the extra insult to injury work required to deliver all the data and internal knowledge to this external consultant.

The "whys" of the need to go outside could be one or more of the following:

- An interest to get an outside or independent view of what drives the business.
- The analytics group is too busy with other core functions.
- The analytics group doesn't have the capability to do the more advanced analytics needed.
- The analytics group has been too rigid in their findings and is not open to other insights beyond what they've already provided.
- Somebody's returning a favor.
- Internal agenda or effort underway that is only known at the top, and third-party needs to be brought in to keep things confidential.
- Someone at the top wants their theory adopted and someone, some group, and/or the analytics team just isn't quite delivering that message. The third-party will typically endorse what this top individual wants to have presented, with the appearance that this independent third-party discovered it on their own.
- There is an unpleasant task that requires a third party to completely drive the approach so that there is no appearance of bias internally.

One of the more common pitches in the analytics space has been the promise of finding all sorts of new, previously untapped, critical insights. This is nothing new. Some examples going back about 20–30 years ago were Neural Networks and Data Mining. In fact, there was a popular story about a retail chain that analyzed a variety of transactions at their stores. What they found was a most interesting pattern. The sales of diapers and beer had a strong correlation. Supposedly, fathers were sent out on a late-night run to get diapers.[22] They not only picked up diapers but also picked

---

[22] "Diaper-Beer Syndrome," *Forbes*, April 5, 1998, https://www.forbes.com/forbes/1998/0406/6107128a.html?sh=1163b4736260.

up beer. The retailer, using this new insight, made sure to put the beer and diapers near each other. Sales zoomed. This became known as the beer and diapers story. Over the years the truth of this story has been challenged, but it didn't matter. The story's imagery coupled with the potential to mine untapped "nuggets" in data warehouses, launched the data mining movement.

Most recently, you hear terms like machine learning and artificial intelligence (AI). The promise of each one of these is always enticing. In fact, much of the software and methods used behind these approaches are not always something completely new.[23] When someone outside the analytic space hears these terms, they believe that they must adopt this approach. They don't know what exactly the specifics are, but they are very enthused by the presentation or promotional materials they just saw. This is not to say that there haven't been great strides in AI technology, but all the complexities and intricacies of a specific business (and the people who are running that business) are not always easily categorized into the nice clean "business rules" that are required for AI.

As individuals become more experienced both working in analytics as well as working for a specific company, they realize how things work within that particular business. There are all types of knowledge that individuals acquire along the way that they can't necessarily explain to a system. They spend each day making stronger connections and associations with why the business operates the way it does, for better or worse. They also take note of the people in the organization that they work with and what those individuals are looking for.

There are also things that individuals come to know through their analytic experience at the company. For databases that might be where they're located and what's in them. What do you have to watch out for? What data is trustworthy and/or complete? I mentioned in Chapter 1 that someone working with the data just comes to instinctively know that you have to exclude inactive customers before you run an analysis. The company may also have restrictions for doing business in certain states. In many industries there are restrictions on who you can do promotions to and as

---

[23] Mike Lloyd, "Don't Believe the Hype: AI is No Silver Bullet," *Computer Weekly*, August 7, 2020, https://www.computerweekly.com/opinion/Dont-believe-the-hype-AI-is-no-silver-bullet.

a result, those restricted segments need to be suppressed from the analysis and results output. There may be different cost structures on segments, which have to be used when doing an analysis.

These are just a few examples of the experience that is embedded in an experienced internal analytic group. I like to call this "Official Intelligence." Official Intelligence doesn't come overnight, and that knowledge can't be easily packaged in a simple spreadsheet (though many have tried). Official Intelligence is similar to what is also referred to as human intelligence—though I prefer Official Intelligence, as the analysts are and should be, the official experts on the data they work with.

Outside third-parties, especially when they bypass the analytics group, tend to dive into the data analysis with their specific approaches and tend to minimize some of these "endemic to the business" ways of doing things. They are not close to business, are not aware of different data idiosyncrasies and/or restrictions, but they want to prove that their artificial intelligence approach is going to find something much more insightful. They also might feel that they really didn't need the analytics group to help them get there (other than explaining what all the data means). This third-party's first clue was that the analytics team wasn't even involved at the outset.

This is not a great situation, and unfortunately was created by the internal analytics bypass. At some point, both the third-party and the analytics group will need to get aligned.

There are other considerations that are sometimes ignored when using a more sophisticated approach. As I mentioned previously, having some type of black box algorithm that might seem more efficient usually requires an explanation of its specific workings. For the decision-maker to pull the trigger on a certain approach they want to understand it intimately. If that approach is still unclear or too advanced or complicated to explain, or "proprietary," they might not be comfortable.

I recall someone once coming to me internally and asking me to develop a more sophisticated incentive goal algorithm for each sales representative. An incentives sales goal for a sales representative is a number that they are targeted to achieve. Based on how well they do against that goal they get paid a certain amount. After showing them some of the data, this individual thought that a certain type of quadratic function would work well. They even liked the idea that this approach might be "cooler" and more advanced. This was a little more complex than what had been done previously.

The problem came when this approach was communicated to their leadership. While their leadership found the approach might be a little better, the complexity of explaining this to all the sales representatives so they could understand how this quadratic goal worked and why, became a bigger challenge. In short, the benefit of moving to this more sophisticated approach did not outweigh the confusion created from the new incentive model rationale. Ultimately, the approach was not used.

Another example where AI doesn't necessarily have the knowledge is how the final model will get implemented. Many years ago, I worked on a model at a large company. When it came time to execute that model, I had an eye-opening experience.

The exercise was to build a model that would predict an individual's probability of response. Many of the approaches that had been used previously were of the form if X > a, and Y> b, and Z > c then the prospect was contacted, otherwise the prospect was not contacted. The model I built used what is a known a logistic regression approach. For each individual, (i) the probability of response, given I had variables x_i, y_i, z_i, w_i, would be equal to

$$prob_i = \frac{1}{1 + exp^{-(k+ax_i+by_i+cz_i+dw_i)}}$$

Where exp (x) = e^x, e = 2.718281828, and k, a, b, c, and d were constants.

For many modelers this is a familiar equation (and logistic regression ensures a result between 0 and 1, which is exactly what you want when you're talking about probabilities).

What I came to learn is that when I wanted to implement this formula, I was not allowed to "run" the process, (nor could I offer a file that could be matched as an interim step in the process). This had to be implemented on the master database as part of a productionalized process. I had to explain how someone who did the general production code was to implement this process. I explained how the formula worked. The response I got was, "I don't do 'exp's,' whatever that is, and it's not in the code we typically use." They had certain ways of doing things and there was little flexibility.

While I was able to find a happy medium to score every record on the database, it made me aware that the implementation on certain analytic models has to be integrated into a production process. If it's too sophisticated, it will have to be simplified, so those who do the production implementation can code it. If that level of sophisticated code cannot be translated to something in "production-eze," you will have a problem, and all that hard work may be diluted. You can curse all you want as the sophisticated analyst, but it usually won't do any good. Having this official intelligence at the outset will not be understood by the artificially intelligent software.

Another important aspect to consider is that even though you might be excited by exploring an AI approach, there are usually (ad hoc) business initiatives at that particular point in time that tend to override the search for interesting patterns in the data. Executives may be very fixated on specific business dynamics and almost every analytic request is connected with those initiatives. These initiatives take on a certain life of their own in intensity and it is sometimes difficult to connect the AI work with the latest twists and turns of these efforts.

I don't want to sound too negative on analytic consulting support using some type of AI. I've been on both sides, as the head of analytics groups, as well as working at two different analytic consulting companies, so I've seen what tends to work out well.

First and foremost, if you are supported by an internal analytics group, get them involved before you communicate with or bring in the outside AI help. Let your analytics group know what you're trying to achieve and what you're really expecting from an AI effort. It always works better this way and the analytics group, while potentially being resistant and/or defensive at first, will not be blindsided by your interest. You also want to value your own analytic team's feedback. You don't want to find out the hard way about implementation issues/examples mentioned previously, when you're at the end of the AI analytic journey.

If done this way, your analytics group will feel that they are part of the effort. From the analytics team standpoint, they will also get an opportunity to potentially enhance their analytic knowledge. In other cases, the analytics group may be so overwhelmed with the day-to-day ad-hoc work that they would welcome the help. In either case, make sure to let your analytics folks know at the outset.

From the analyst's standpoint, use the opportunity to understand what may look valuable from this AI approach. You may make some important distinctions on what resonates with your clients that you may not have thought about before. This will only make you a more experienced and well-rounded analytics person.

Based on my experience, I would advise internal clients not to discount some of your analytics group's official intelligence in favor of the artificial intelligence. In many cases, it comes down to asking better, clearer, and more precise questions. Give some hypotheticals like, "If I found something like this, what would the action be?"

There is always room for more sophisticated and potentially efficient approaches. The balance of these with those who not only know the business, but the analytics of the business, makes for the most optimal mix.

CHAPTER 16

CRACKING THE CASE

When we last left our marketer and analyst after the meeting debrief, they uncovered the following to explain the slow-down in sales:

- Their competitor sources most of their business from Arizona.
- A number of their top customers are from that area.
- A former executive of the company, Pierre Poacherre, joined the competitor as head of marketing. He is based in Arizona.
- The salesperson who was assigned to the Southwest area previously left our company and appears to have joined this Pierre at the competitor company.
- The marketer and analyst have since let the head of sales know of this situation, a day prior to going into the meeting. They conferred as to the best-recommended next steps. The head of sales is very appreciative of the beforehand heads-up.

As the analyst and marketer walk into the follow up meeting, they have a very different approach to the presented material. The focus is now on the problem at the hand, which was a slow-down in sales (the "what"). The main reasons for the slow-down appear to be a combination of not only a recent sales person's departure, but that this individual has joined forces with another former employee. This former employee is now the head of marketing at this competitor. All of this happened in the Southwest, where it turns out, the head of marketing is now based (the "why"). They also both know our top customers and caught us flat-footed.

As the meeting begins, the top executive in the room, the franchise head, is digesting all of this material and the findings. As he is nodding, he says, "This is great work! Do you have recommendations as to how you think we should proceed? The marketer and sales head have both reviewed the top customers and plan to travel to Arizona in person to connect one-on-one where possible. The top exec says, "I totally agree." He also offers to come as well if they think it will help. He mentions that he knows one or two of these customers and that he will reach out, as well (the "how").

As the meeting comes to a close, the top executive says, "Good work again folks. Good teamwork. Let's turn this situation around."

While I've changed some of the details, this situation is actually something I experienced firsthand. As the picture started to develop and the data started to point to where the insight was, I was amazed at how presenting focused analytics combined with the knowledge of different folks in the organization who were closest to certain aspects of the situation, garnered real action. In fact, the situation was turned around positively, and our brand never looked back.

This experience has always stayed with me. It was a great feeling as an analyst and what you should hope to strive for.

As an analyst, the analytic detective work never ends, but make sure every so often you take a step back to appreciate your contribution.

ACKNOWLEDGMENTS

I first want to thank my wife Wendy and my son Matthew for supporting and cheering me on throughout this whole process. I couldn't have done it without them. I also can't forget my mom and my sister for their enthusiasm throughout this endeavor, as well. I also want to thank my dad, who passed away in 1997. He said to me before he passed that I would get my book written one day, and not to worry. Twenty-four years later, it's finally happened.

I want to thank Gary Simon, whose advanced probability and statistics course I took at Stony Brook in the late '70s made such a big impression on me, that I realized statistics was a lot more interesting than what was portrayed in most of the textbooks at that time. As I was interested in pursuing further study in statistics at graduate school, Gary had recommended a colleague of his. They both went to Stanford where they both received their doctorates.

I took Gary's advice and went to the University of Connecticut where I studied statistics for my Masters and PhD under Alan Gelfand. Alan, who is known worldwide for his groundbreaking work in Bayesian Statistics, was a tremendous advisor for me. I was very fortunate to study under such a brilliant individual who always challenged me to get to the next level.

I'm also indebted to the UConn Department of Statistics staff back then, who made me feel like family in their graduate program and had the confidence in me to be a lecturer in the department for both introductory and advanced statistics courses. In addition to Alan Gelfand, I want to also thank Uwe Koehn, Tim Killeen, Bruce Johnson, Dipak Dey, Nitis Mukhopadhyay, Dolly Smith, Lynn Kuo, and Joseph Glaz. I can say that it was one of the few times in my life that I couldn't wait for the weekdays, because I so enjoyed learning there.

I also want to recognize Ojars Lasmanis, who couldn't have been a better boss in those heady days in downtown Manhattan at American Express. He knew everything there was to know about American Express and mentored me on how to really think about and present analytics on the big stage at Amex. He also had tremendous enthusiasm and was ahead of his time in the ideas he shared with me.

After Ojars left Amex, I considered taking the scary leap into starting a statistical modeling company. While this was an exciting thought, I wasn't going it alone. At Amex, I led the non-customer acquisition modeling group and Sam Koslowsky led the customer modeling group. Together, we formed a company called The Marketing Investigators (aka TMI Associates). I am very thankful to Sam for being part of this endeavor, which was in business for close to eight years. This experience was incredibly valuable.

There are three individuals I met when I started working in pharma analytics who have always given me great guidance wherever I was, and have become my life-long friends.

First, I can't say enough about Tom McCourt. Working with Tom is the most enjoyable part of my career. His knowledge and versatility have always impressed me. He has also been one of my greatest supporters. There are few people you just connect with in business, and for me, Tom has been one of those rare individuals. When I first started out in pharma, I was at a company that I had second thoughts of staying with, after only three weeks. Tom saw what I was trying to accomplish and went out of his way to let me know he had my back. Since that time, I've never looked back, and I owe a huge amount of my success to Tom.

Second, I'd like to thank both Mike Nanfito and Kurt Habel, who have always been there to help me navigate through some very challenging business problems. Their good common-sense instincts, as well as their innate business know-how, have been incredibly valuable to me.

There are many others during my pharma analytics experience who have been a great part of my success and I want to recognize them: Paul Rabideau, Darcy Christel, Len Kanavy, Kurt Graves, Mark Iwicki, Rob Tallman, Cheryl Gault, Mark Plinio, Margie Stelwagon, Cathy Miller, Dan DeForge, Kimball Tarr, Michael Karbachinskiy, Paul Johnson, Jorge

Blum, and Steve Kurzeja.

Last but not least I can't forget Book Launchers, Collective Next, and Frank Cozzarelli.

Book Launchers is the main reason this book finally came to fruition. I had been talking about writing a book for way too long and I never could follow through. I realized I needed help. When I saw videos online from Book Launchers with Julie Broad, I knew this could be what I'd been missing. Best decision I ever made. The whole Book Launchers team is absolutely great! Every step of the way Book Launchers was there to guide me. Their depth of knowledge about all the components of the book-writing and book-launching process is astounding. I can't thank them enough.

Collective Next is a company I was exposed to at a company off-site. They are a consulting company that helps organizations navigate through a wide variety of challenges. They deploy a process they call "graphic facilitation" where "they draw what they hear in real time." I made a mental note at the time that I wanted their help when the time came. I want to thank Brett Saiia, Matt Saiia, Sara Shrimplin, and Jeff Amidei. Collective Next is responsible for all the great animations inside this book.

Finally, I want to thank my good friend Frank Cozzarelli. Frank was incredibly helpful behind the scenes, providing me with invaluable advice, while making sure I didn't forget any critical details.

CPSIA information can be obtained
at www.ICGtesting.com
Printed in the USA
BVHW080950021121
620548BV00004B/96

9 781737 308102